Appraisal Procedures
in the Secondary Schools

DONALD J. BROWN
California State College at Hayward

Prentice-Hall, Inc., Englewood Cliffs, New Jersey

Foundations of Secondary Education
Jean D. Grambs, Editor

P: 13-043612-7
C: 13-043620-8

Library of Congress Catalog Card Number: 74-104175

Current printing (last digit):
10 9 8 7 6 5 4 3 2 1

Prentice-Hall International, Inc., London
Prentice-Hall of Australia Pty. Ltd., Sydney
Prentice-Hall of Canada Ltd., Toronto
Prentice-Hall of India Private Ltd., New Delhi
Prentice-Hall of Japan, Inc., Tokyo

Printed in the United States of America

Foreword

The average person asked to react to the word "judge" formulates a picture in his mind of a black-robed personage who sits high above a court where justice is dispensed. Not many individuals would conjure up the picture of a teacher. Yet teachers act as judges every day they teach.

The tools teachers use for judging are many: tests, observations, and rating sheets. Every child who has gone through the American school system has been tested literally thousands of times. He has had judgments made about his competence in spelling, singing, jumping hurdles, understanding Shakespeare, determining the area of a circle, and listing the elements of a cat's nervous system. There are few items in educational experience which have been more subject to the pen of the cartoonist than the youngster bringing home a report card. The report card is in effect the sum of the teacher's many judgments.

Teachers try to be fair. They hope their tests measure what they have taught. They hope they have assessed competence objectively. Yet these are difficult things to do. The new teacher is typically overwhelmed by the job of adequately evaluating student performance, and he is often deeply distressed by his new role of judge. The judging role is particularly critical since a single teacher's judgment can mean an open door to further opportunity, or the loss of significant future achievement.

The preparation of teachers allows only a small amount of time to be spent acquiring this critical skill. Dr. Brown's book is designed to provide supplemental help for the teacher in training who does not have extensive class time provided. Because Dr. Brown has constructed this volume on the basis of what his students indicated they need to know both before and after student teaching, the book is uniquely practical. It is not designed to make statisticians nor sophisticated researchers out of future teachers. Rather, it is designed to help all teachers do a more adequate job of objective evaluation, so that both teacher and student have a mutual understanding of standards.

The need today is for assessment that is professionally conducted, which helps both student and teacher humanely diagnose areas of need as well as areas of progress. Dr. Brown's book helps the beginning teacher to achieve this goal by providing a wealth of examples, and a rare sense of humor.

JEAN D. GRAMBS
University of Maryland

Preface

This book is intended to help teachers, or prospective teachers, acquire and understand the principles and procedures that will allow them to do a more effective job in evaluating student achievements.

All too often, texts in this field attempt to arm the student with an overabundance of theory and mathematical manipulation which is seldom understood or really that necessary for the typical classroom teacher. The main thrust of this book has been to present in simple and uncomplicated language just those principles and procedures that are necessary for the development of classroom tests and the utilization of these results. This approach is one, I hope, that will increase the reader's understanding and usage rather than confusing him with psychometric jargon.

Much of the content and structure for this book was provided by actual teacher and student comments gleaned from over 400 taped structured interviews in Alameda, Contra Costa, and Santa Clara Counties in California. These comments are sprinkled throughout the chapters. Special thanks are due to the graduate students who conducted these interviews in 1968.

An acknowledgment is also due Professor Tudor Jones, who was my coauthor on this book until his work commitments became such that he was unable to continue. Our preliminary meetings and discussions proved invaluable as this book developed.

My indebtedness to the authors and publishers who gave permission to reproduce materials from their works is gratefully acknowledged. Appreciation is also expressed to Jean D. Grambs for her valuable suggestions as the book progressed. A special acknowledgment is due to Mrs. Rose Burgis, who typed the final copy. Finally, it is a pleasure to acknowledge the assistance of my wife, Charlyne, who read the preliminary drafts and offered valuable suggestions. Without her support and assistance this book could not have been completed.

DONALD J. BROWN

Contents

9 ASSIGNING GRADES: THE PARADOXES, THE INEQUITIES, AND THE PLAIN TOMFOOLERIES, 103

10 PUBLISHED TESTS: AN EVIL OR A BLESSING? 118

11 A LOOK INTO THE FUTURE, 144

APPENDIX I: A GLOSSARY OF MEASUREMENT TERMS, 152

APPENDIX II: COMMONLY USED PUBLISHED TESTS, 168

INDEX, 178

1

The Encounter:
Teachers and Students

Most teachers and students are willing to discuss their ideas and feelings concerning the way students are judged and evaluated in their school. With few exceptions, a discussion in this area usually stresses three categories: teacher-made classroom examinations, grading practices, and the value of published tests. The viewpoints expressed in each area are as different as the person who makes them, but they do provide a realistic point of departure for the study of appraisal techniques in the junior and senior high schools.

THE STUDENTS

Students become quite verbal when discussing classroom examinations. Their comments reflect not only what they consider a "fair" test, but also those things that they have come to expect from exams after being exposed to many different teachers and teaching methods during their school years. The fragments below show the diversity of views about classroom tests.

Ask more specific questions. Sometimes I'm pretty vague about what she is asking. An example of this is, "Show how the author brought out the main theme." If you have lots of themes running through the book you might pick the wrong one and spend all your time going off on a tangent. (12th Grade, English)

Sometimes he asks tricky questions, you know, to try and get us confused. I don't like that idea. He should ask what we've been learning, what we've studied. (9th Grade, Fine Arts)

If the teacher wants to help the students, the tests are fair. (8th Grade, Spanish)

Often times we don't have tests for weeks at a time. When the tests are given, only two or three questions are used to cover all the reading material. (12th Grade, American Government)

His tests measure what we know or should know by giving us problems very similar to what we've been working on. We do not expect something to be put on the test that is not being studied at the time. (10th Grade, Geometry)

We have timed tests that measure how fast we type, but we never are tested on things like do we know how to type a business letter. That's just homework assignments. (10th Grade, Typing I)

Sometimes they're hard to understand. (7th Grade, Core)

He doesn't take any questions out of the next chapter on stuff we haven't had. He gives review sheets before the test to help us study. (9th Grade, General Science)

Her tests are on what she's gone over. If you've listened, you can pass the tests. (11th Grade, Physical Education)

The purpose of the classroom examination is to estimate how much each student has learned of the material being studied, and students feel this purpose should be reflected in all of the teacher-made tests. Vaguely worded or tricky questions are confusing and, as a result, the students do not show how much they know of the material, but rather how good they are in trying to figure out what the teacher wants. Generally speaking, students in the junior and senior high schools expect classroom examinations to include questions that cover the material that they have been studying.

Final grades are a source of concern for all those in school. "How do teachers arrive at final grades in your class?" "Do you think they indicate how much you know of the subject?" and "Would you change the grading system if you could?" are questions that have been asked of students many times. Secondary school students have varying viewpoints. Below are some typical responses to these questions.

I could do without grades but you have to have some sort of way to know whether you graduate or not. I kind of like the idea of pass or fail. It would be easier to argue that you've done enough to deserve to be passed in the class. Sort of a reward for the suffering every day. (12th Grade, English)

Just because you flunk a course doesn't mean you don't know the work. Sometimes you didn't turn in all those goofy assignments. (10th Grade, Life Science)

Sometimes they ask questions you don't know and you might know some other questions that they don't ask. (9th Grade, Fine Arts)

Shouldn't be averaged the way they are. Should give us more credit for improvement. Encourages us to try harder. (12th Grade, Homemaking)

If you eliminated grades there would be no guidelines for other teachers. You need them to know how you measure up to other people. (9th Grade, High Math)

I don't like to study so I get bad grades, but I know more. (10th Grade, World History)

He uses per cents—90 per cent and up is an A and so on. He gives us tests and oral quizzes. On the quizzes we can use our notes but they don't count as much as the tests. (9th Grade, General Science)

Who knows? She says so much for tests and so much for homework and so much for classwork but she gets a lot of other stuff in there. If you talk in class or don't pay attention or don't know the answers, you've got big trouble. (12th Grade, Social Studies)

It would be great not to worry about grades then you wouldn't, all the time, have to explain to your parents why they're not so good. (12th Grade, General Math)

Homework and tests decide your grade and if you're on the borderline, your class participation. But it is mostly your test grades that determine your grade. (10th Grade, Geometry)

Most students have learned to accept the teachers' judgments, in the form of grades, as an established part of our educational system. They are, however, very much aware of the many shortcomings of this practice.

Periodically a published test, usually an achievement battery or an intelligence test, is administered in the schools. The administration of a single battery can take up to ten hours. The values assigned to these tests by the students vary considerably. Many students take them in stride, many become bored, and others become emotionally upset, but the majority try to do their best. Here are some typical comments.

You stayed in there too long. You're real fresh for an hour or so, but after that you're real tired. You really don't know what you are doing. (9th Grade, Algebra)

I don't know. What good are they? They're too long. Sometimes I get to just seeing spots from looking at those answer sheets. But I usually try. (11th Grade, English)

I play tic tac toe all the way down—see if I can finish first. Not interested. Can't see what history has to do with your life's work. I'm not going to be governor. (11th Grade, Metal Shop)

I try to do my best but I sort of feel like a robot because the questions they seem to ask are about something you can mark on a scoring sheet, not something you can talk about or express your feelings. (11th Grade, History)

They should explain why we are taking these tests. (8th Grade, English)

They're just something you have to do. (11th Grade, English)

Like it was easier than going to classes and at least something different. It took a long time and I was doing the questions kind of sloppy by the time we got through. (12th Grade, English)

They're a headache. You have to take them if you have

to. I am always nervous and scared. I can't eat. (10th Grade, World History)

Thought it was fun. I did real good. (7th Grade, Core)

The tests are great. Taking one test a day is okay. However if you take all the tests in one day, after a couple, drawing those little bubbles makes you tired and you don't really care. (9th Grade, Algebra)

Most students take these published tests during the school years without having a clear idea as to the tests' values and purposes regarding their total educational program. As a result, the scores that many of the students receive are not good indications of their achievement in broad curriculum areas or their ability to undertake the different types of high school programs.

THE TEACHERS

In order to look at another side of this question of student evaluation, a number of teachers from a wide variety of teaching areas were interviewed. The interviews centered around the three basic discussion areas—the classroom examination, grading practices, and use of published test results—which the students had identified. Their opinions did not vary as much as the students' views, but they did indicate there is no universal approach to appraising students in classes.

The classroom examination is generally looked upon as an important instructional aid. The degree to which teachers use an examination as such varies. The following comments point out differences in teachers' views of classroom tests.

Teacher-made tests get you out of a lethargic position. When I make up my own tests, I have to be realistic with what I've given the kids. I'll direct what I am teaching to those questions. (8th Grade, English)

I think students can learn while they're taking a test, giving them items about which they must think. I also feel that learning is greatest on going over a test. (12th Grade, Social Studies)

I think you can make a test that will lead students through the redevelopment of ideas or concepts that you have tried to develop in class. It helps to get ideas straight and forces the students to put ideas into categories. (10th Grade, Geometry)

They show whether or not you have reached your educational goals. (7th Grade, Core)

I use mine as a teaching device. I try to put as much in the test as kids can learn from. (10th Grade, World History)

Yes, they show you where you've failed to get the point over to the students. With the way we're organized in the department as to book use, though, you don't usually get a chance to go back and pick up the pieces. (12th Grade, English)

The student listens to you in class because he knows he is going to be tested. He is not going to learn anything unless he reads. So if testing forces him to read and listen, then perhaps it is really an instructional aid. (11th Grade, English)

You're giving the test not only so you can tell how much the student knows, but also so the student can see if he's kidding himself, if he thinks he can do all these things and he can't. (10th Grade, Typing I)

Tests are too often used just to get a grade. The kids, of course, think this too. When you take a test, the only reason you take it is to get a grade; not as a learning process. But it can be used as a learning process and I try to. (7th Grade, English/Social Studies)

The interviewed teachers are generally aware of the importance of the classroom examination as an instructional aid. Many feel that the test itself is a learning device. The degree to which they use the examination as such varies with the teachers' concepts of what they want the students to know, recall, apply, or synthesize after a period of instruction.

Determination of the grades earned by a group of students is a personal thing among most teachers. No two teachers will calculate it exactly the same way. Even with a school or district policy, variations among the teachers are great. Just how do teachers perform this very important function? When asked their bases on which grades were given, a group of teachers responded with these answers.

Precision of work, attitude, and behavior. I don't use a curve. I grade each student individually. (11th Grade, Metal Shop)

Represents a combining of tests, daily work, class response, and attitude. All of these are averaged for each student. (12th Grade, American Government)

I use a point system—around a standard deviation and the mean. Sometimes a simple system of arranging in order and dividing. (11th Grade, United States History)

I average homework grades, quizzes, and tests. I ask myself if this grade really represents what the student seems to know. I adjust it as necessary. (9th Grade, Pre-Algebra)

I record test and other grades in different colors. Major tests are recorded red. Other grades in blue or black. Quiz grades are numerical, all others are letter grades. I average up all numerical grades and establish a curve on those. Then I assign letter grades to the numerical grade. For this they get a red letter grade. The quiz grade is used to determine borderline grades. It's difficult because English grades are really subjective. (11th Grade, English)

I use an adjusted curve. I go through and figure up the total number of points possible, then I figure the student's standing on a per cent basis. I consider test grades, oral quizzes on reading assignments, class participation and conduct, and whether a student has improved. (9th Grade, General Science)

I grade on a percentage of possible points basis—90 (A), 80 (B), 70 (C), 60 (D). I give points for tests, quizzes, and homework. Borderline students are considered individually on their class participation and attitude in class. (10th Grade, Geometry)

I work it strictly on a four-point system. I transfer the letter grade into numbers, add the points up, and divide the number of grades into the number of points and then determine what the grade will be. Then my subjective evaluation plays into it. (8th Grade, English)

It is apparent that a variety of grading practices are being used by the teachers interviewed. Grading on a curve, an adjusted curve, averaging all assignments, a point system, and a percentage system are all represented. To each, his own procedure is the best and fairest method of determining students' grades.

Teachers were asked, "In your opinion, what are some of the important values of published tests to the classroom teacher?" The teachers interviewed were all of the opinion that these types of tests were useful, in varying degrees, for the classroom teacher. The extent to which the results are used is expressed in the following comments.

Only as an indication. Possible potential. I use them sometimes to get a better understanding of a student's performance. There are so many factors involved when they are taking the test, I just don't know how important they are. I've seen students take them and a lot of it is hit and miss, guesswork, etc. (8th Grade, Spanish)

They give you someplace to start in evaluating students and whether they are working up to their ability. Also they help place students in the proper class for their ability. (10th Grade, Geometry)

Probably they can substantiate what you already know or have observed. (12th Grade, United States History)

To establish a frame of reference for looking at the class —that is, pointing out strengths and weaknesses which will alter teaching methods. (7th Grade, Core)

The primary value of them is, when I suspect a student is not capable of handling the work, I can come in and check his scores on a test. I never use the test scores unless the student is a problem. (11th Grade, English)

The test gives you an idea of the capabilities of the students. Teacher observations and judgments are of more value in rating and understanding the students. (8th Grade, History)

I don't depend upon them very much. They do give me an indication, yes, but sometimes the indication is misleading, because some kids test poorly; like on an intelligence test, it's based on reading. If they don't read well, they don't test well. (7th Grade, English/Social Studies)

They give a basis, or some indication, of what a teacher can expect from each student. (9th Grade, Fine Arts)

From the above comments, it is apparent that the teacher's use of published test scores is limited. The teachers are aware that these scores give an indication of the capabilities of each student, but generally use them only to supplement their judgments concerning one or more of their students.

A METHOD OF ATTACK

The first two sections of this chapter have presented some interesting views of the appraisal techniques now being used in schools. The diversity of opinion, both within the teacher group and between the student and teacher groups, is obvious. The one idea commonly agreed upon is that appraisal of students is an expected and essential part of education. Exactly how this evaluation is to be accomplished is open for debate.

In recent years, there has been a great deal of discussion of the use of appraisal techniques in the classroom. It is beyond the scope of this book to present all the pros and cons of the issues involved, but an attempt has been made to offer a sound and defensible position in many of these controversial areas. It is hoped that you will approach these areas with an open mind, questioning and searching for the "right way" for *you* and not just accepting what is written because it is in print.

For those who desire to read additional and more detailed treatments of these controversial areas, a short list of selected references is included at the end of each chapter. These references were chosen to provide you with the opportunity to look through and study the wide variety of viewpoints expressed in many of the standard textbooks in this field, as well as in some more advanced books that focus on specified areas.

As you read this book you will notice that the chapter titles are different from those normally used in textbooks. These titles represent student viewpoints concerning the chapter topic, teachers' concerns and viewpoints, or the author's general feeling about an area to be discussed. The chapters are grouped to present the information necessary for a basic knowledge of educational testing. The major groupings are those discussed by the students and teachers in the two earlier sections of this chapter.

Beginning with Chapter 2, the teacher's responsibility to the students in regard to classroom examinations is discussed. What is the teacher's responsibility for easing the student's emotional excitement during an examination? Should he understand why students cheat on tests? How can students be prepared for taking an exam? Should the corrected examination be used as a teaching tool? Such questions have been the subject of much discussion and controversy for a number of years. The position taken in this chapter is that the teacher has the responsibility of helping students look at tests positively, i.e., tests should be used to identify not only what is known, but also those areas in which further instruction is necessary for a better understanding of the material.

Chapter 3 discusses the general characteristics of educational measurement. The answer to the question, "How do you know whether an examination is good?" involves the concepts of validity and reliability. An understanding of these concepts is important for those who develop and use tests in the classroom.

Chapter 4 takes the point of view that classroom testing is an essential part of the teaching process. In other words, teacher-made tests should reflect instructional objectives. A step-by-step procedure is presented for designing a classroom examination.

Chapters 5 and 6 present the characteristics, advantages, and disadvantages of the essay and objective question formats. Numerous examples are presented to illustrate the points covered in each of the chapters.

Chapter 7 suggests ways an objective test can be put together and analyzed. Examples of these areas include: the order of questions, preparation of the scoring key, clarification of the directions, and the general test format. Also included in this chapter is a discussion of item difficulty and item validity which is designed to help the teacher analyze each of his test questions.

Chapter 8 discusses the statistical treatment of test data. The statistical methods explained and the statistical computations presented are those which seem typical for the average classroom situation in which the teacher's primary concern is measuring and evaluating the progress of students.

Chapter 9 is devoted to the problems associated with assigning grades to a classroom of students. "What are the purposes of grades?" "Do final grades indicate how much a student knows of the subject?" and "Are there sex differences in the grading practices being used?" are some of the questions answered in this chapter.

Chapter 10 deals with the two most commonly used types of published tests, i.e., achievement and intelligence. Their strengths and weaknesses are discussed. Examples of test questions from both an achievement and an intelligence test have been included for study.

Chapter 11 provides a look into the future of educational measurement. This chapter discusses the exciting breakthroughs toward improved instruction that are made possible by the recent development of some new technological devices. With the impending increased instructional use, the secondary teacher should be aware of the potential each of these devices offers for improving his appraisal of student achievement.

2

The Better I Teach, the Better My Students Will Do on My Examinations

As a teacher, have you ever been thanked by a student for giving him an examination? Probably not, but each student should be grateful for the time that you spend developing it, scoring it, and discussing the results so that you and the students may discover what has been learned and areas in which further instruction is necessary.

In many schools, however, the announcement of an examination sets up "battle lines" in which student and teacher try to outwit each other. Students in a situation like this have, through the course of their school years, been conditioned to dislike and often fear examinations. To many students tests are a threat; even the best students fear failure, or fear that they may not do as well as they think they should.

The importance of tests in determining grades is well known to the student. A great deal of anxiety is often built up in preparing for the exam, taking it, and discussing its results in the classroom. Students often know the answers but are unable to figure out the meaning of the questions, or later can't understand why points were taken off their grades.

These issues will be looked at in the rest of this chapter. The views presented together represent one position; the reader should examine each issue critically.

THE TEACHER'S RESPONSIBILITY

I give a lot of surprise tests in my classes. They really keep the kids motivated to do their homework.

If they pay attention in class and do their outside assignments they should know everything on the test.

I always give a review sheet that covers the most important things in the unit or chapter before the test to help the kids in their studying.

Just what is the teacher's responsibility to the students in regard to classroom examination? There is little agreement among the teachers currently working in the schools. Student comments offer some insight into this question, as shown by the following.

Those "pop" quizzes are for the birds. Man, you never know when to expect them. They're awful.

Well, in the beginning, we didn't pay attention to things she said in class, and didn't know it would be on a test later. But now I pretty well know what she's going to ask on a test and I can study better for it.

If you don't study the review sheet it's your own fault, and if you don't study you are going to get a bad grade.

Generally, students feel that a scheduled classroom examination that covers the materials discussed in class and in the assigned readings is "fair," both for the student and for the subject matter covered. In other words, it is the teacher's responsibility to help the student, in every possible way, get the best possible score on any examination, i.e., to teach him so that he will learn as much as possible and do as well on the exam as he is able.

Many teachers take the opposite viewpoint. They pride themselves on the difficulty of their tests, and do not feel an exam was any good if many students made high scores. The reason for this viewpoint is difficult to determine. Some may feel that their fellow teachers will not respect them if their course is too easy.

Others may feel that lowering of standards so that many students do well is the curse of present-day education and, therefore, they maintain possibly spurious high standards by making "tough" exams that few can pass.

Generally speaking, most students consider classroom examinations a necessary evil. Students possessing a positive attitude toward tests are few and far between in the secondary schools. Negative student feelings about tests have been built up over a number of years, and will undoubtedly take a long time to change. With some students, test taking will never become a challenging and learning experience. For the majority of students, however, it is surprising how much change of this feeling can be accomplished in a few months. Several approaches that can be used to develop more positive attitudes are presented in the remaining sections of this chapter.

Easing Emotional Tension during the Examination   Students often get overly excited just before an examination. Before entering the classroom, they hurriedly compare notes as to possible answers to such and such a question. The frantic give and take between partially informed and mistaken students produces a feeling of insecure preparation and serves to impair the student's ability to think. To overcome this, some students delay their arrival until the last minute, with the result that they are often late and miss the opening directions. Other students have learned that if they arrive early for the exam, they can keep calm and collected by engaging in small talk with the person sitting next to them.

In order to avoid emotional excitement during the exam, the teacher should offer certain suggestions. The first step is have the student glance through the entire exam to get some idea of how long it is, the types of question formats used so that adequate time can be reserved for essay questions, and to see if certain parts are worth more points than others. The second suggestion should point out that the student should go through and answer all of the questions that are easy for him, and then return to those questions for which he did not know the answer. In most cases, all of the objective type questions are not equally easy, but usually have the same point value. Therefore, it is better to work on many easy ones and omit a few hard ones than vice versa. The last suggestion to ease the emotional excitement during an exam would be just to do the best that he can. Every student would like to get every question right, but the tests are usually made difficult enough to give a range of scores, and no one is expected to answer all questions correctly. This is a point the teacher can stress.

Understanding Why Students Cheat on Examinations   Teachers have different methods of handling the problem of cheating during examinations. Some make a big production out of it: dramatically marching down an aisle, snatching the exam paper from the desk, ripping it into shreds, and announcing to all that the student's grade is zero. Others may virtually ignore it, telling themselves that there was insufficient proof of cheating. Most teachers, however, become quite disturbed when cheating is suspected, and the penalty for being caught is usually quite severe.

Cheating on exams is not new; there are indications that the practice is increasing at all grade levels. The majority of students want to earn good grades and in some cases are under considerable pressure to do so. As a result, they resort to cheating. How many of you have cheated? In any case, the teacher should understand why some students will resort to this practice, and should make every effort to decrease the pressure so cheating will not occur while exams are being taken.

Rather than decreasing the pressure that leads the student to cheat, teachers have tried a number of techniques to curb cheating entirely. One system that has questionable value involves a statement at the end or beginning of the exam which the student signs, indicating that he has not cheated or will not cheat. The underlying assumption is that students will control their impulse to cheat if they realize that they have to sign such a statement. This system has not done much to curb the practice of cheating, but it has increased the number of cheaters who make false statements. A commonly used extension of the "honor system" is to have the students report, in writing at the end of the exam, the names of students they saw cheating. The extension encourages the "roving eye" technique of cheating, disturbs the students' concentration on the task, and creates a police state atmosphere which is highly undesirable, and also does not work.

A better method is for the teacher to eliminate all unnecessary temptation to cheat by seating students in positions from which they cannot see one another's papers. If this is impossible because of limited facilities, the teacher can prepare two or more forms of the exam, so that students sitting side by side will be working on different items. This practice is used by a tenth-grade geometry teacher who says, "Use two copies of the test. A student has to do his own work. The answers are different but the concept is the same. I think more teachers ought to use this." Generally, two forms of the tests are developed by taking one test and rearranging the order of items so that all students will answer the same questions, but in a different order.

The best way to decrease the pressure to cheat on an exam is to prepare the students properly in advance of the testing period. This involves a clear explanation of the instructional objectives that will be included on the examination. In addition, teachers should inform the students of opportunities for extra work or special testing in case they don't do well on the test. One twelfth-grade history teacher explained an experiment she conducted in one of her classes.

> The students and I discussed an experiment in testing and grading. We decided that the experiment would consist of giving tests from time to time. Any student who got 70 per cent or better passed. Those who didn't had opportunities to retake the test until they passed it. Any student who took the test again could not get higher than a C. The students who got 70 per cent or above could do extra work to raise their grades.

Using this method, the students begin to realize that the teacher is in the business of teaching what needs to be taught, and not there just to assign grades. Most students would rather not cheat on an exam and will not if they know that they can raise their grade by availing themselves of other opportunities.

Preparing Students for Examinations　　Basically, the scores the students make on your examination are a reflection of your teaching ability, i.e., "the better I teach, the better my students will do on my examination." In order to provide the best possible learning situation, the teacher should spend considerable time in identifying which of his teaching objectives will be included on the exam. After determining those skills and abilities which will be tested, he should give the students the list of objectives. Using it as a guide for their studying, the students will be engaged in a meaningful and challenging learning experience.

As an example, a Tests and Measurement teacher is preparing an examination covering a unit on the construction of teacher-made tests. He identifies those objectives that will be covered on the exam and gives them to the students so that they may direct their study into these areas.

1. Know the technical terms of the unit.
2. Know the basic steps in constructing an exam.
3. Know the various types of question formats.
4. Know the advantages and limitations of each type.
5. Be able to write good exam questions of each type.

In addition to giving the students a list of the skills and abilities to be included on the exam, a teacher with students who are unfamiliar with his testing methods should give examples of the types of questions they will be asked.

(T) F   It is a desirable practice to announce that a test will "get at" certain specific objectives of the course.

The function that can be appraised better by an objective question than by an essay question is:
a. To create essentially new patterns of thought.
b. To use language to express one's ideas.
c. The abilities to select, relate, and organize.
d. The abilities to understand and apply factual knowledge. (keyed)

In this way, student feedback will tell the teacher whether the students know how to handle this type of question, and also if they know the content covered by the question.

Giving Examinations Frequently   Because of the time involved in planning an examination, many teachers give very few exams. This limited number of exams places an undue amount of pressure on the students, because failing one could mean an average or below average grade. It is, in addition, questionable whether a teacher can get an accurate rating of the amount a student has learned with only two or possibly three exams in a four- or five-month period. Most students would prefer to be tested more often so that they know where they are and what areas need more studying. A ninth-grade student sums up this need: "I'd like to have weekly tests so I could know what I'm doing and see how much better I have to do."

The learning atmosphere in a classroom will improve if the students realize that frequent examinations will be given to check on their learning progress toward the objectives of the class. The teacher should, however, point out that these exams will be used to identify not only what is known, but also those areas in which further instruction is necessary for a better understanding of the material. With this atmosphere, the students usually feel less pressure and more motivation to learn.

Using the Corrected Examination as a Teaching Tool   The majority of good teachers return scored examinations as soon as possible, usually a day or so after they have been taken. The returned exam provides the opportunity for detailed discussion by the teacher and student—why the correct answer *is* correct, what the teacher expected in the way of an answer, and the reasoning required to answer each of the questions. This practice is best identified by a student's comment, "She goes over the test completely and you can ask questions if there is anything you don't understand."

An eleventh-grade girl's comment characterizes a less desirable practice: "He doesn't go over them very well and there isn't much you can do." All too often, teachers spend their time in justifying to the students why they received their grades. As a consequence, the students look at their scores, compare notes with other students, argue with the teacher that a certain grade is unfair, or brood on the thought that they hate exams.

"Learning is greatest on going over a test. I've experimented and found this use of tests as teaching material really works. I've retested after a review of the test with remarkable success." This high school social studies teacher characterizes still another dimension. He goes on to say that his approach toward reviewing the exam to promote the greatest amount of learning is changed each time. He makes a special effort to obtain student feedback for improving his review. The following example illustrates the importance of knowing how students feel. In this illustration, a teacher presents her method and two of her students offer suggestions for improvement.

> *Teacher*:   I tell each class the number of A's, B's, etc., in the class, and read them a sample of an A paper and stop to make comments along the way on what it has in it that was expected and well done.

> *Student*:   It would be better if she'd put a list of stuff she wanted in the answer upon the board so we could get an idea of how to go about it the next time we had a test.

Student: I'd rather have an average (C) paper read with all the good and bad things pointed out so you could judge your own a little better. An A paper only has good points and you never find out what's bad about writing in certain ways.

This practice of using the returned exam as a teaching tool provides the student with very valuable information. In addition to pointing out the correct answer, what the teacher expected in the way of an answer, and the reasoning required to answer each question, the student can gain a great deal of insight into future examinations. What kinds of questions were asked: definitions? interpretations? problems? discussions? Were they primarily from the assigned readings or from class discussions? Were they the expected questions? What was wrong with the answers given: not complete enough? poor distribution of time on the important parts of the test? questions omitted? careless mistakes? What suggestions did the teacher write on the exam for improving the answer? If the teacher discusses the returned exam with these in mind, a very interesting and profitable learning experience should result, and much can be done to modify the attitude expressed by a high school senior: "Once it [the test] is over, who wants to worry about it?"

After discussing the returned exam, some teachers immediately collect them and deprive students of the opportunity of learning the things they missed. A tenth-grade typing student said, "After the test, she could prepare another ditto, like a worksheet, so we could take it home and study the things we missed. Otherwise, we just look at the score and never learn the things we missed." The primary concern of these teachers is the security of the exam questions. They realize that other students will have access to them, and the exam will not be able to be used again. This is true, but hardly an educational disadvantage. If these questions are looked at and studied by other students, a good deal of learning may result. One of the best ways of preparing for an exam or a class is to look over and study questions that the teacher has used on past exams.

Other teachers do not worry about examination security, and would agree with the following comment from a teacher.

I find that I can't use the same exam over again because my teaching changes from one year to the next. You know your general points are always the same but you may emphasize something one year and not the next. It's not fair to the kids.

Many of these teachers use their old exams as a method of preparing their students for the first classroom examination. They provide sufficient numbers of previously used exam questions so that students can look at them prior to all of their examinations.

SUMMARY STATEMENT

This chapter represents just one point of view regarding the use of examinations in the classroom. Many people will challenge this point of view because it is contrary to many traditional methods now being used in the schools today. This fact should not force acceptance or rejection of any method. You are urged to look at both sides, think about them, and then decide the best way for you to use examinations in your classroom.

SUGGESTED READINGS

Bloom, B. S., "Testing Cognitive Ability and Achievement," in *Handbook of Research on Teaching*, ed. N. L. Gage. Chicago: Rand McNally & Co., 1963, Chap. 8. Discusses the changes that take place in students as a result of different learning experiences.

Ebel, R. F., *Measuring Educational Achievement*. Englewood Cliffs, N.J.: Prentice-Hall, Inc., 1965, pp. 208–211. Discusses the causes and cures for cheating on classroom tests.

Robinson, F. P., *Effective Study* (rev. ed.). New York: Harper & Row, Publishers, 1961, Chap. 4. This chapter outlines some of the ways students can prepare themselves for examinations. Many of these ways can be used by the teacher to prepare his students.

Stodola, Q., and K. Stordahl, *Basic Educational Tests and Measurement*. Chicago: Science Research Associates, Inc., 1967, Chap. 3. Discusses possible ways for teachers to change students' attitudes toward classroom tests.

Tyler, R. W., "What Testing Does to Teachers and Students," in *Testing Problems in Perspective*, ed. A. Anastasi. Washington, D.C.: American Council on Education, 1965, pp. 46–52. An article dealing with approaches for making student attitudes toward testing more positive.

3

How Do You Know Whether
an Examination Is Good?

Every day our lives are touched by measurement in one of its many forms. For example, a high school student gets up at a certain hour by the clock, takes a shower that he regulates for the proper amount of hot and cold water measured by a meter, and dresses in clothes that are sold by sizes. He usually eats a breakfast of eggs (sold by the dozen), toast (sold by the loaf), and milk (sold by the quart). He glances at the clock, jumps on his bike, and arrives at school just before the last bell, which is rung by the clock in the main office.

Throughout the day he attends classes that are 50 minutes long, and has a five-minute break between each of them to get from one class to the next. At lunch time he buys a hamburger and a milkshake which he pays for with money from his weekly allowance. During his fifth-period class, he takes a classroom exam that has 40 questions and will be measured in points. After school, he returns home to still more forms of measurement.

These common experiences are characteristic of the

emphasis placed on measurement in our modern world. Since appraisal of student achievement is a form of this measurement, let's take a closer look at it.

GENERAL CHARACTERISTICS OF EDUCATIONAL MEASUREMENT

Noll has summarized some of the general characteristics that apply to measurement in education.[1]

1. Measurement in education is quantitative. By use of educational measurement we get scores, norms, IQ's, averages, and so on, all of which are numerical expressions.
2. Error is present in educational measurement. As we gain knowledge and experience in a field, our measurement techniques improve, the margin of error decreases, and the results become more exact. As workers in any subject area learn more about measurement they develop an attitude of suspended judgment.
3. Educational measurement is generally indirect rather than direct. The weight of an object can be determined directly in pounds and ounces. By contrast, educational measurement is indirect. We do not measure such traits as intelligence or mechanical aptitude directly, but rather by inference. As an individual is able to perform designated tasks, we are able to draw from the results of his performance certain conclusions about his intelligence or aptitude. The same is true for school achievement.
4. Educational measurements are relative. There is no unit of achievement in arithmetic, no unit of aptitude in music, no unit of school intelligence which is comparable to absolute zero, or centigrade, or time of the earth's rotation. Standards of educational measurement are based on observed performance of typical students.

Teachers generally ask many questions about an examination. How can I make an exam that will give me a true picture of each student's achievement? How much confidence should I have in the scores of the test? What are some of the things that can affect the students' scores?

Despite the many different types of test question formats,

[1]Victor H. Noll, *Introduction to Educational Measurement* (Boston: Houghton Mifflin Company, 1965), pp. 10–11.

there are certain important general characteristics that all examinations should have. These are validity, reliability, and factors influencing validity and reliability.

If the classroom exam used by the teacher incorporates these important characteristics, then he is justified in employing it with his students. An understanding of these characteristics is necessary before they can be incorporated into a classroom exam.

Validity

The validity of an exam or a question on the exam is determined by the extent to which it actually measures what the teacher intends it to measure. In other words, a valid classroom examination measures what has been taught. How, then, can a teacher-made test fail to be valid? The answer to this question is, quite simply, "there are many ways."

There are several ways of looking at the validity of a test. Textbooks usually identify content, criterion-related, and construct validity, each of which requires a different type of evidence of validity. Two of these methods, content and construct, are of particular importance for classroom examinations. The other type, criterion-related validity, refers to the predictive or diagnostic quality of a test, and is usually not considered an appropriate criterion for teacher-made tests.

Content Validity   This type of validity indicates the extent to which the exam covers the material the teacher has taught and the way it was taught. This statement implies that a valid test provides for measurement of a good sampling of content and is balanced with respect to the teacher's emphasis of the various parts of the subject matter.[2]

How is it possible, then, for teacher-made tests to be weak in content validity? Unfortunately, it is in this respect that many classroom tests are weak. For an example, many teachers under the pressure of time or inexperienced in writing exam questions turn to the teacher's manual of the textbook they are using, and select test questions from those the author proposes. These questions usually reflect the objectives of the author and his emphasis on certain sections within the book. The teacher, on the other hand, may have different objectives and have emphasized differ-

[2]For a more thorough discussion of this topic see pp. 29–40, which deal with the construction of a Table of Specifications.

ent areas. Thus, the resulting exam may not truly focus on what the student has been expected to learn in the classroom.

Another way a teacher-made test can be weak in content validity is through the use of the wrong question format. If a teacher is interested in obtaining a measurement of students' knowledge of factual information in American History, the use of essay questions would limit the content validity of the exam. An essay exam only has three or four questions, and this limited number of questions affects the number of topics that can be included on this type test. Use of objective-type formats, e.g., true-false, multiple-choice, and matching, allows a greater breadth of coverage of facts. The teacher should be aware, however, that unimportant material may receive the same emphasis as the important content on the exam. Care should be taken to ensure that this does not happen.

The decision as to how many questions each of the sections or topics of a course should have on the exam is another area that influences content validity of a teacher-made test. The balance of content in an exam reflects the degree to which an instrument parallels the materials which have been taught and the way in which they have been taught. Certain sections or topics are less important than others, and the number of test questions should reflect this importance.

It should be pointed out that a classroom exam may have adequate content validity at a given time for a particular class and teacher, but may not be equally valid for testing another group which had a different teacher. In addition, it would be well to keep in mind that the content validity of an exam is a changing characteristic. It must be examined each time the same test is given to a new group of students.

Construct Validity   This refers to the kinds of learnings specified or implied in the objectives. Construct validity, as well as content validity, should be considered in evaluating classroom exams. As pointed out above, the content validity of a teacher-made test is judged on the basis of how adequately it represents the total content of a given instructional unit. Construct validity, on the other hand, concerns the test's ability to measure the student's actual achievement of the instructional objective. For example, look at the following three objectives of a high school course:

  1. The student should know the terminology of the unit.

2. The student should be able to explain in his own words _____.
3. The student should be able to apply knowledge of _____.

Each of these three objectives requires different types of learning, and each is dependent upon the preceding one. The first objective requires the student to recall information covered in the course, such as dates, names, and places in social studies. The second objective is a different type of learning, and at a higher level. In order to satisfy this objective, the student has to know the terminology of the unit and have a good understanding of the course materials so that he can explain orally, or in writing, those aspects of the course materials specified in the test questions. The third objective reflects yet a different type of learning. In order to satisfy this objective, the student should know the terminology of the unit and have a good understanding of the course materials. Within the third objective, the student may be asked to apply what he has been studying to a new, or novel, situation. This objective, therefore, has the student use this information in a situation different from that in which it has been learned.

The teacher should take into consideration that different kinds of learning are involved and that different examination tasks are needed to measure them. A classroom examination should be so constructed that each kind of learning can be tested. Only in this way is a valid measurement of student achievement provided.

Throughout this section, we have been referring to a "valid" test. We have stated that subject matter, objectives, and students must be taken into account when judging the validity of a classroom examination. It should be pointed out, however, that validity is not an either/or situation. It is a relative term, and in each exam there are degrees of validity. A high degree of validity in each exam is a goal toward which all teachers should aim.

Reliability

The reliability of an examination is the degree of consistency with which it measures what it is supposed to measure. That is, a reliable test gives consistent results. For example, if a test is given once and then readministered to the same group of students, each student should get about the same score on both administrations. Teachers generally ask, "Why should I be concerned with reliability, since I never give the same test to my students a second time?" Even though an exam is not used in this way, teachers should be aware of the following points concerning the nature of reliability and the exam characteristics which promote consistent results.

As was the case with validity, one cannot simply say that a test is, or is not, reliable. There are degrees of reliability in the test results. A statistical measure of reliability can be obtained by comparing the scores earned by a student for different administrations of a test, or may be computed by determining the degree of relationship between the student's scores on the odd-numbered and the even-numbered questions on the test. (These procedures will be discussed in Chapter 8.) The reliability coefficient indicates by means of a decimal the relationship between these two sets of scores. In other words, a perfect relationship is indicated by a coefficient of +1.00. No relationship between the two scores would have a zero coefficient (.00). The higher the numerical relationship between the two scores, the greater the reliability.

Teachers rarely sit down and compute a reliability coefficient for a classroom exam. They are more concerned with controlling as much as possible those factors that can affect the reliability of their tests. The following factors provide some clues for ensuring maximum reliability in the design of a classroom test.

1. *The quality of the test questions affect reliability.* The exam questions should be so stated that the students understand exactly what is wanted in the way of an answer. If they are not clearly stated and are misinterpreted, the reliability is affected.

2. *The length of the test affects reliability.* In general, the longer the exam, the greater the reliability. A short test (around five or six questions) cannot spread the students' scores sufficiently to give consistent results. Therefore, the more we sample the students' knowledge, skills, and understanding, by using a number of questions, the more reliable our appraisal of each student's achievement will be.

3. *The difficulty level of the test affects reliability.* If the test is too easy, all of the students will score very high. Conversely, if a test is too difficult, the scores will tend to bunch at the lower end of the scale. In both cases, we cannot determine how much each student knows. A difference of one or two points can't reveal a true difference in achievement. Only when the test scores are well spread can they clearly show differences in achievement.

4. *Scoring procedures affect reliability.* Another way to make

a test more reliable is to be consistent in scoring it. A scoring key should be prepared in advance for objective questions. If completion or fill-in type questions are used, judgments by the teacher as to what answer is acceptable must be made prior to scoring. The problem of reliability in scoring essay questions will be discussed in Chapter 5.

5. *The testing environment affects reliability.* The classroom should be free from distracting noises and movement. These, along with extreme changes in the weather and even a broken pencil point, can affect a student's performance.

6. *The students' emotional state affects reliability.* Many students approach an exam with varying degrees of emotional excitement. This excitement tends to impair their ability to show how much they know. Teachers should structure their examinations so that this excitement is kept at a minimum.

Factors Influencing Validity and Reliability

In addition to the important qualities of validity and reliability, other factors can influence the effectiveness of an examination. The teacher should be aware of and consider the following points.

1. Directions indicating to the student what he is supposed to do with a question or series of questions and where he should record his answers should be written on the exam paper. They should be clearly and succinctly stated.
2. The test questions should be arranged on the page so that they are easily readable. Also, each question should be entirely contained on one page.
3. All corrections should be made *before* handing out the exam paper to the students.
4. If the examination is reproduced, it should be inspected for readability before it is distributed.
5. In most cases, the test should present the easier questions first. This arrangement tends to encourage students to do their best.

SUMMARY STATEMENT

A classroom examination is good when it is as valid and reliable as it can be made. A valid test not only covers the content of the learning sequence but also measures the kinds of learning which are specified by the instructional objectives. A reliable test gives scores in which the teacher can have confidence. It should be remembered that neither reliability nor validity is an either/or thing. They are both relative terms, and in each exam there are degrees of reliability as well as of validity.

SUGGESTED READINGS

Anastasi, A., *Psychological Testing* (3rd ed.). New York: The Macmillan Company, 1968, Chaps. 5, 6, 7. A clear, practical discussion of reliability and methods for determining and utilizing validity data.

Downie, N. M., *Fundamentals of Measurement* (2nd ed.). New York: Oxford University Press, Inc., 1967, Chap. 4. A presentation of the characteristics and computation of reliability and validity coefficients.

Gronlund, E., *Constructing Achievement Tests*. Englewood Cliffs, N.J.: Prentice-Hall, Inc., 1968, Chap. 8. An excellent discussion dealing with reliability and validity as they relate to classroom testing.

Lindeman, R. H., *Educational Measurement*. Glenview, Ill.: Scott, Foresman & Company, 1967, Chap. 3. A clear presentation of the importance of validity, reliability, and usability to the classroom examination.

Noll, V. H., *Introduction to Educational Measurement* (2nd ed.). Boston: Houghton Mifflin Company, 1965, pp. 77–103. Clearly illustrates the qualities that differentiate a good test from an inferior one. Along with reliability and validity, he discusses objectivity, ease of administration, ease of scoring, and ease of interpretation.

Thorndike, R. L., and E. Hagen, *Measurement and Evaluation in Psychology and Education*. New York: John Wiley & Sons, Inc., 1963, Chap. 7. Qualities essential to every measurement procedure are discussed under the main headings of validity, reliability, and practicality.

4

What Should Classroom Tests Measure?

> In my first experience in teaching I tried to fol-
> low the curriculum guide and all the things that
> were in there and wept regularly on Sundays
> because I hadn't gotten done the things I wanted
> to. (11th Grade, English)

Many teachers, old and new, realize that there is so
much to be taught, so much that would be of value for
people to learn, and so little time to learn, that they
become overwrought with the prospect, as the above
example points out. How then can the teacher define
in specific terms those things a student should be able
to do after a course or a unit of study? This question
is primarily a curriculum one, but it also is basic in
evaluating student achievement. Not only do specific
instructional objectives determine the content and
teaching methods a teacher uses; they also determine
the nature of the classroom exam as well. In other
words, the specific objectives define what we are to
teach, and the appraisal procedures we employ tell us
the degree to which our instructional goals have been
reached by our students.

THE STUDENT AND INSTRUCTIONAL OBJECTIVES

The above relationship can be looked at from the point of view of the student as well as that of the teacher. If the student knows he should, for example, "be able to recognize _____," "be able to explain _____," or "be able to interpret _____," he knows specifically what he is trying to learn. He can devote his time and energy to the task at hand, rather than resort to memorization and mechanical completion of exercises.

There are some teachers, though not the majority, who furnish this type of specific information to their students. The remaining students are faced with the task of studying blindly or "casing" the teacher. The following illustration points out how vague objectives can be interpreted by students in a number of ways, with the result that they have little meaning for the students' understanding of the teacher's desired instructional goals. Three students from the same twelfth-grade social studies class were asked what they thought their teacher was trying to teach them.

> *Student 1:*   All the stuff about government and how all the pieces fit together and who does what. Oh man!

> *Student 2:*   I guess about the government and how it works and why it works that way.

> *Student 3:*   The fundamentals and basics of the course. You know, know what you are studying.

In contrast, their teacher considered the following to be his *specific objectives.*

1. Ability to think an idea through to a logical conclusion.
2. Understanding of basic concepts rather than minute facts.
3. Self-confidence in expressing their own ideas.

These objectives become usable in the evaluation process when they are rephrased into descriptions of the abilities and behaviors that the student is to develop during this unit of instruction. For example, the third objective, "self-confidence in expressing their own ideas," could be rephrased into a specific behavior that the student is to develop: "ability to express concerns orally or in writing for an individual or a group being deprived of the rights guaranteed by our constitution." These specific written descriptions of what the student should, in varying degrees, be capable of doing after a given learning experience provide the teacher with an exact meaning and direction for his teaching and for the construction of his classroom examinations.

POORLY STATED SPECIFIC OBJECTIVES

Most teachers, when asked to state their specific instructional objectives, give statements directly from study or curriculum guides. These statements are usually too vague to provide a foundation for test construction and must, therefore, be rewritten. An example of typical statements from a guide would be:

> To give an over-all view of man's artistic development from 3,000 B.C. until now. (9th Grade, Fine Arts)

> To become a responsible citizen of the United States. (8th Grade, History)

The first statement provides no basis for the measurement of student achievement. Certainly a classroom examination should not attempt to measure what the teacher has done in the way of lecturing, demonstrating, or other means of providing instruction. The evaluation of student achievement can only be carried out by determining what the *students* can do.

The second statement represents the philosophy of the school more than an instructional objective. This very worthwhile statement cannot be measured as a result of a single course or unit. It is, in addition, questionable whether this type of aim can be accurately measured by a paper and pencil test. Such an assessment can only be made after a long period of student development.

Another difficulty in using objectives stated in study or curriculum guides as a basis for classroom examinations is illustrated by this statement.

> To be able to think logically. (9th Grade, Algebra)

No basis of measurement is provided by this statement. The end result of instruction must be specified. In other words, what will the student be able to do at the end of the course to provide us a measure of his ability to think logically? These situations must be specified so that examinations can be developed to measure them.

Another difficulty is shown by the following statement.

The ability to use commas. (10th Grade, English)

This statement is much more specific than any of the preceding ones, but it is still rather broad for testing purposes. How can we determine whether a student can "use" a comma? To use a comma when? In what situations? To reveal ability to use what rules?

Since evaluation must be based on student performance, it can only be planned and carried out when you know exactly what the student should be able to do. The way a student may exhibit this behavior may take many forms. It may be displayed by listing certain facts, reciting given principles, or writing an explanation of some event or phenomenon. It may take the form of demonstrating some manipulative skill, performing some physical feat, or displaying some desirable social behavior. In other words, statements of objectives must include the exact behavior that the student is expected to exhibit. They should tell what the student is to be able to explain, recite, solve, and demonstrate.

CRITERIA FOR STATING SPECIFIC OBJECTIVES

If specific objectives are to guide the teacher in deciding what is to be taught and what is to be evaluated, attention must be given to the way in which these objectives are stated. The following criteria are suggested as guides to be used when writing such statements.

1. *Statements of specific objectives should be worded in terms of the student.* The evaluation of achievement is carried out by determining what the pupil can do. In meeting this criterion, it is often helpful to preface the specific objective with the words, "The student should." For example, the student should:

1. Recall the six basic classes of food.
2. Recall the common sources of these classes of food in their diet.

2. *Statements of specific objectives must include the exact behavior that the student is expected to exhibit.* The application of

this criterion means that the objectives will not contain such terms as appreciate, understand, or comprehend, but rather be stated in terms of what a student will be able to do. For example, "The student should be able to recall _____," is better than, "The student should understand _____."

3. *Statements of specific objectives must be in specific terms.* The test for this criterion is that the wording be sufficiently specific and clear that another person reading the objective would derive the same meaning as the person who wrote it.

4. *Statements of specific objectives must be realistic to the grade level.* What has the student already learned? What is the student ready for? Only when we have answers to these questions do we know whether or not certain objectives are appropriate for the student's next stage of development.

5. *Statements of specific objectives must be attainable in the course or unit.* An objective such as "develops an abiding interest in civic affairs beyond the years of formal schooling," if used by a twelfth-grade social studies teacher, provides little help in guiding him as to what he should do with or look for in the student right now.

A DESIGN OF A CLASSROOM TEST:
AN EXAMPLE

> I am a high school social studies teacher and am developing an instructional unit on the structure of Brazilian slavery and its bearing on ethnic and social conditions in modern Brazil. In general, I want my students to know the following things after a two-week unit:
>
> 1. Knowledge of important terminology.
> 2. Knowledge of specific facts.
> 3. Knowledge of sequences and trends.
> 4. Knowledge of the impact of slavery on the population of modern Brazil.
>
> What is the next step in developing a classroom test?

The above represent the first step in the development of a test; the teacher has identified the main ideas or general objectives which he wants his students to learn. The second step is to divide each of the general objectives into specific objectives, which, when taken together, would show growth toward the general objective. At this stage, the crucial question the teacher must ask himself is, "For this grade level, what are the exact and specific things in which the student should show growth?"

The following specific objectives represent the information, the concepts, and the ideas that the teacher has identified for inclusion in his unit classroom test.

The student should: Know the important terms.

1. Recall the difference between the "Vertical" founders and the "Horizontal" founders.
2. Define the term "miscegenation."
3. Recognize the differences between the terms "mulattoes" and "mamelucos."

Know specific facts.

1. List the causes of miscegenation.
2. Recall the dates of slavery in Brazil.
3. Recall the two sources of slaves.
4. List the reasons why slavery in Brazil was considered less harsh than in the United States.
5. Recall the estimates of the number of Negro slaves imported.
6. Compare the percentage of the population in various ethnic groups in 1822 with what it is today.
7. Describe the living conditions of the planters and of their Negro slaves.
8. Be able to describe the role of the frontiersmen in the enslavement of Indians.
9. Recall and list all of the major social and ethnic conditions that are characteristic of modern Brazil.

Know sequences and trends.

1. Develop a knowledge of how two major forces gradually stopped the enslavement of Indians.
2. Understand the continuing influence of slavery on the attitude of the planters toward manual work.
3. Describe the gradual merging of the frontiersmen into the frontier.
4. Explain why the majority of Brazilians today are of "white stock."
5. Explain how Brazil earned the reputation of the most licentious country in the world.

Know the impact of slavery on modern Brazil.

1. Know the influence of miscegenation on Brazil's music.
2. Describe the racial problem in Brazil.
3. Recognize the aristocratic prejudice and disdain for manual work.
4. Refute Stockard's theory that interbreeding among widely different human stocks has caused degradation, elimination of certain groups, and loss of intellectual and social power.

The identification of these specific objectives provides a guide for the instruction itself, and ensures content validity of the test for the unit. Using these as a base from which to work, the next step is making an outline of the content to be included in the teaching unit. The outline should include the major content areas as well as the subareas under each of the major areas of the unit. In addition, the amount of time planned for each of these areas should be shown. This amount of time can be expressed by the number of days that will be devoted to each, or by percentage of the total time of the unit for each area. Following is a possible content outline for the high school social studies unit.

Content Outline: The Structure of Brazilian Slavery and Its Bearing on Ethnic and Social Conditions in Modern Brazil —1530–1888 (abolition of slavery). Two weeks

I. Introduction (one day).
   A. Portugal proceeded to establish her control in Brazil, May 8, 1500.
   B. Development of the sugar plantations, and later the coffee industries.
   C. Two types of colonists in Brazil: The *Vertical* Founders—the sugar cane planters; and the *Horizontal* Founders—the frontiersmen or "bandeirantes."
II. Plantation System. Just as Negro slavery and cotton and tobacco grew up together in the old South in the United States, so Negro slavery and sugar, and later coffee, grew up in Brazil, where the planters were political lords. The sugar cane planters built for themselves big stone or brick houses—called "big houses." The slave quarters were given an African name—"Senzalas."
   A. Enslavement of Indians in plantations (one day).
   B. Importation of Negro slaves from Africa (1530's– 1850's) (two days).

1. No exact figures available. Estimates range from 3 to 18 million.
2. Used to tropical climate and adapted easily to Brazil.
3. Planters develop an aristocratic attitude toward manual work.
4. Planters had Negro mistresses and the offspring were the "mulattoes."

III. Frontiersmen (one day).
   A. At first, bold pioneers in search of gold and Indians to sell the planters as slaves.
   B. Without wives, they intermarried with Indian women. The children were called "mamelucos."
   C. Later they settled in the frontier, continued to intermingle with the Indians, and with the Negroes when sugar plantations with their slavery moved westward.

IV. Miscegenation (interbreeding of races): The interbreeding of the Portuguese and Negro elements with one another and with native Indians gave Brazil an outstanding example of social and ethnic democracy. By 1822 (Independence) it was estimated that half her population was full blooded Negro. Of the 80 million people of today's Brazil:
   60% are white
   30% are mixed blood
    8% are Negro
    2% are Indians
   A. Causes of miscegenation (two days).
      1. Iberian peoples for centuries were used to thinking of a dark-skinned race (Moors) as masters of a large part of the Iberian Peninsula.
      2. The theory of Indian as a noble savage.
      3. Lack of European women in Brazil.

V. Treatment of the slaves (one day).
   A. The life of slaves in Brazil struck foreign observers as being less harsh than in other countries having Negro slaves.
      1. Brazil resembles in climate much of tropical Africa from which the Negroes came.
      2. The Portuguese, a people of mixed origins, generally are less color conscious than the English, French, or Dutch.
      3. The Portuguese seem to have inherited from the Moors the domestic rather than the industrial system of slavery (slave was part of the family).

VI. A traumatic experience (two days).
   A. The amalgamation of races does not support Profes-

sor Stockard's theory that mongrelization (interbreeding of races) among widely different stocks has caused degradation, elimination of certain groups, loss of intellectual and social power.

1. The large number of Brazilian writers, architects, painters, composers, and medical scientists in tropical diseases and anti-venom serums refute the theory of an inferior civilization that should be prevailing in Brazil.
2. The largest number of political leaders and men of scientific and artistic talent are from Brazilian areas of more intense ethnic amalgamation.

B. Owners of slaves developed aristocratic prejudice and disdain for manual work, effects today reflected in class distinction.
C. The abuses of miscegenation dragged down Brazil's moral plane. It earned and has never entirely lost the reputation of the most licentious country in the world.
D. Fraternalism, indolence, and moral prejudice, though in a small degree, still prevail today.

At this point the "test design" begins to take the form of a chart showing a complete content analysis. The following table represents the suggested test plan for the proposed unit. In the left-hand column, the five major content areas are listed, along with the percentage of instructional time alloted to each major area. Across the top of the chart are the four general objectives that were drawn up by the teacher. The major elements of the content of the unit are listed under each of the appropriate objectives. The number of test questions that the teacher plans to use for each unit are also entered on the test plan. These parenthetical entries represent the teacher's decision as to the kinds of learning to be tested. At the bottom of the test plan, the total number of test questions for each of the objectives are listed to allow the teacher to check for any imbalance in the general test plan.

The final task in the preparation of the test plan is to determine and specify the number of questions which will be written for each teaching unit of the test plan. This, of course, is controlled by the number of items in the exam itself, which depends in part on the time available for testing and the ability of the group of students in your class. Other factors to be considered include the type of question format that will be used, the complexity of these questions, and the type of objectives being tested, i.e., questions dealing with knowledge of terms will require less

Test Plan: The Structure of Brazilian Slavery and Its Bearing on Ethnic and Social Conditions in Modern Brazil

Objectives and Content	Knowledge of Terminology	Knowledge of Specific Facts	Knowledge of Sequences and Trends	Impact on Modern Brazil
Plantation system 35%	vertical founders "Senzalas" "mulattoes" (three or four items)	1530's–1888 enslavement of Indians importation of slaves (1530's–1850) estimate of number 3 to 18 million Negro adapts easily to climate (six items)	enslavement of Indians attacked by churches; antagonized the Indians planters develop attitude against manual work planters had Negro mistresses and the offspring were the "mulattoes" (four items)	influence in music, sports, dialects, architecture class distinction (two items)
Frontiersmen 10%	horizontal founders "Bandeirantes" "mamelucos" (three or four items)	search for gold sell Indians to planters as slaves (two items)	intermarried with Indians settled in frontier areas intermarried with Negroes when sugar plantations moved westward (three items)	development of the frontier (no items)
Miscegenation 20%	miscegenation social and ethnic democracy (two items)	causes of miscegenation: lack of European women; theory of Indian as a noble savage; Iberian peoples ruled by dark-skinned Moors percentage of the population in 1822 and today in various ethnic groups (six items)	Negroes and Indians disappearing, merging into the white stock (two items)	distinctive feature of Brazilian civilization has been the interbreeding of Portuguese and Negro elements and with the Indians (three items)

Treatment of slaves 10%	(no items)	less harsh treatment of slaves in Brazil similar climate Portuguese less color conscious domestic rather than Industrial system of slavery Adoption of mulattoes by Portuguese (four items)	time of abolition of slavery (1888), Negroes merged into society with little difficulty (no items)	race relations not a major problem (one item)
Traumatic experience 25%	Professor Stockard's theory (one item)	still exist in Brazil class distinction fraternalism indolence racial prejudice (two items)	Brazil earned and has never entirely lost the reputation as the most licentious country in the world. (two items)	The largest number of political leaders and men of artistic and scientific talent are from Brazilian areas of more intense ethnic amalgamation. (three items)
Total number of test questions (based on a 50 item test)	10 items	20 items	11 items	9 items

complexity than an objective test dealing with knowledge of sequence and trends.

Theoretically, a teacher builds an examination which can be answered in the allotted time. It is usually also planned so that students will not dawdle on any question. But to complicate the point further, each student has a different rate for answering different types of questions. Perhaps the best guide to appropriate length is afforded by the teacher's own experiences with the class. For most classroom exams, it seems desirable to adjust the number of questions so that at least 80 per cent of the group can finish the entire test. As a rough rule of thumb, you should include no more than 50 objective-type questions in a 50-minute period. However, it may be necessary to alter this number in accordance with the complexity of the questions themselves and the reading level of the class.

In our illustration, a test of 50 questions has been planned. The number of questions to be written for each cell has been determined to reflect the teacher's decision as to their relative importance. Adjustments in the number of questions might be necessary if you encounter difficulty in writing questions in any given cell. Care should be taken that sufficient questions are written to permit an adequate sampling of the students' performance in all of the important specified course objectives. The test plan is of great help in making sure that a close relationship exists between the content and objectives of the unit and the classroom examination based upon them.

SUMMARY STATEMENT

Teachers should attempt to obtain the closest possible relationship between the aims and purposes of a given instructional unit and the classroom examination used to measure those aims. This chapter has pointed out the need for stating specific objectives, and their importance in developing a classroom examination.

SUGGESTED READINGS

Ahmann, J. S., and M. D. Glock, *Evaluating Pupil Growth* (3rd ed.). Boston: Allyn & Bacon, Inc., 1967, Chap. 2. A thorough discussion covering the areas of identifying the needs of youth, translating needs into educational objectives, the taxonomy of educational objectives, and formal statements of educational objectives.

Bloom, B. S., *et al.*, *Taxonomy of Educational Objectives: Handbook I: Cognitive Domain.* New York: David Mc-Kay Co., Inc., 1956. A discussion of the problem of classifying educational objectives in a systematic way. The cognitive domain includes those educational objectives dealing with recall of knowledge and the development of intellectual abilities and skills.

French, W., *et al.*, *Behavioral Goals of General Education in High School.* New York: Russell Sage Foundation, 1957. This is a report of the specific objectives of the general education program in the secondary school.

Greene, H. A., A. N. Jorgenson, and R. J. Gerberich, *Measurement and Evaluation in the Secondary Schools* (2nd ed.). New York: David McKay Co., Inc., 1954. The latter half of the book consists of separate chapters on measurement in the commonly taught subjects in the secondary schools. Each chapter presents statements and discusses objectives in the subject field.

Krathwohl, D. R., *et al.*, *Taxonomy of Educational Objectives: Handbook II: Affective Domain.* New York: David McKay Co., Inc., 1964. A volume dealing with the classification of educational goals in the noncognitive domain.

Lindvall, C. M., ed., *Defining Educational Objectives.* Pittsburgh: University of Pittsburgh Press, 1964. An excellent collection of articles concerning all aspects of educational objectives. The ideas that are presented should prove stimulating and contribute to the clarification of thinking on this topic.

Mager, R. F., *Preparing Instructional Objectives.* San Francisco: Fearon Publishers, 1962. Techniques for stating objectives explicitly in behavioral terms are presented. Examples of well stated and poorly stated objectives are included.

Remmers, H. H., N. L. Gage, and J. F. Rummel, *A Practical Introduction to Measurement and Evaluation* (2nd ed.). New York: Harper & Row, Publishers, 1965, Chaps. 7 and 8. An excellent discussion of educational objectives with suggestions on how to formulate them, and illustrations of objectives of various types.

5

The Developing and Scoring

of the Essay Question

The essay question has been damned by test experts for many years, but praised by humanists. It is still probably the most widely used format in secondary school classroom examinations. Criticisms directed toward the essay question are based, for the most part, on the questions currently being used in the schools.

> As I visit schools now and examine everything that teachers are doing to appraise what their students have learned, I cannot point to a single important change from the measurement practices of 1935, when I first began visiting the 30 school systems that were involved in the Eight-Year Study. . . . These tests rarely get at anything more than knowledge and skills. When they try to get at anything like creativity, imagination, appreciation, critical thinking, or attitudes, they usually come a cropper. . . . No competent investigator would use these grades as evidence of what the students have learned, but they pass as coin of the realm even though we all know that many are worthless.[1]

[1] P. B. Diederich, "Cooperative Preparation and Rating of Essay Tests," *English Journal* (April, 1967), 573–574.

If, however, essay questions are used for the purpose for which they are best suited, are clearly written, and are rigorously scored, these questions have no equal as a measuring device.

CHARACTERISTICS

The essay question gets its name from the manner in which the student responds. The word "essay" implies a written response that may range in length from one sentence to a paper requiring the whole class period. When scored, it requires the teacher to make a judgment regarding its quality and completeness.

Many students would rather answer an essay question than an objective-type question.

> In essay questions, you can express your true feelings about the question, plus whatever the teacher wants in the answer. (12th Grade, Government)

> I think I like essay best. I like to write and it gives me a chance to pull things from the teacher's lectures, my notes, and the book. (8th Grade, Spanish)

When students were asked if they studied differently for an essay-type exam than they normally do, they replied as follows.

> Yes I do, when it's an essay on a chapter or unit I read the chapter thoroughly 3 or 4 times, but when it's objective I usually study by skimming through, then reading through the important parts. (11th Grade, Science)

> I study the underneath part of the book; the things between the lines. For an objective test all you have to do is study the facts. (8th Grade, Literature)

These students are expressing the significant features of the essay test. They welcome the opportunity to be able to organize their answers and express them in their own words. In this way, they are able to indicate to the teacher just how well they know the material.

In addition to these significant features, the essay question has several important advantages. These may be summarized as follows.

1. The student is less likely to get the correct answer by guessing. In the essay test the student is required to organize and write his own ideas in response to the question, rather than to recognize the correct response from those presented in an objective-type question, or to respond to clues that have inadvertently been left in the question. In other words, the essay question can provide a more valid measure of student achievement than objective-type questions.

2. The format is appropriate for measuring objectives dealing with "relationships," "comparison of two or more things," "cause or effect," "application of rules or principles in a given situation," "analysis," or "critiquing a theory or position." The essay question is also suitable for the evaluation of such essential skills as being able to organize and defend a certain position. It also provides the teacher with evidence of the student's ability to express his ideas clearly in writing.

3. The essay test requires less time to construct than the objective test, since there are fewer questions in an essay exam.

While the above advantages should be kept in mind, the teacher should be aware of the limitations connected with the essay format. These are summarized below.

1. The most obvious limitation deals with the scoring of this type of question. Since it can be scored only through a judgmental process as to its completeness and quality, the consistency of scoring each paper is difficult to maintain. (A later section in this chapter will deal with this limitation.)

2. The time needed for students to answer each essay question limits the number of ideas that can be tested in a class period. This suggests an inadequate sampling of content. In other words, a good sampling of content requires many questions.

3. Even a short essay test requires a great deal of scoring time. While this type of exam is more easily and quickly made, the scoring of the answers is very time-consuming.

In reading through this section, one may come away with the idea that essay questions are more suitable for the students in high-ability classes rather than those in the average or slower classes; those in the academic classes rather than in the general or terminal classes. It is true that the brighter students respond better to this type of question, but the other, larger group of high school students should be given ample opportunity to learn how to organize and write out ideas, attitudes, and feelings during their school years.

GUIDELINES FOR GOOD ESSAY QUESTIONS

Once a teacher has decided that the essay format represents the most effective way to measure the students' achievement of course objectives, he usually asks, "How can a good essay question be distinguished from a poor one?" The following are the commonly agreed-upon guidelines to follow in constructing good essay questions.

1. Phrase the items so that they are clearly stated and students have no difficulty in understanding what is required. A general rule is to use the simplest possible wording that will convey the desired meaning.
2. Relate the test to the instructional objective of the unit to ensure maximum content validity.
3. Make sure that the question is measuring objectives *other than* knowledge or specific facts which can best be tested by objective-type questions.
4. Keep the number of questions and the time required to answer them within reasonable time limits so that the students can demonstrate their abilities.
5. Present the students with an interesting and challenging problem.
6. Write the questions so that they are of such range of difficulty as will allow all students to demonstrate their level of mastery of the question.

Perhaps the most common error in writing essay questions is to require students to "discuss" something without providing a basis for the discussion. For example, a science teacher may ask, "Discuss the development of sponges." The student must make many decisions as to what will go into his answer. Should it include where they grow, how they are made up, the various kinds, significant uses, how they relate to their environment, what do they feed on, or what feeds on them?

A better way to phrase this question so that each student will interpret it the same way would be:

Explain how each of the following influences the development of sponges.
A. Where they grow.
B. How they relate to their environments.
C. Their structure.
D. Their source of food.
E. What feeds on them.

The rephrased question sets a more common base for the students' answers. It does, however, break one question (the original one) into five, and will require a relatively long time for the answers to be written.

Another error in writing essay questions is starting the question with such words as "list," "who," "what," or "when." These words are likely to present a task requiring the student to give forth factual information which can best be measured by an objective-type question. It is much better to use words such as "contrast," "compare," "give reasons for," or "explain how or why." These words will help present tasks requiring the student to select, organize, and apply his knowledge in his written answer.

"In your opinion" or "what do you think about" are phrases commonly used on teacher-made essay questions. It is surprising how often the teacher using such phrases is not really interested in the students' opinions or feelings, but is more interested in determining whether the student knows what the teacher said or what was in the textbook. The only time these phrases should be used is when the purpose of the question is, for example, to get an expression of attitudes, or to determine how logical a defense a student can make of the position he has taken. In the former instance, this expression of attitude really cannot be graded. In the latter, the teacher should be interested not in the position the student took, but in how well the student defends his position.

PREPARING STUDENTS TO TAKE
ESSAY EXAMINATIONS

Each type of examination requires unique skills and has its special difficulties. The most common error made by students in answering an essay question is to waste time writing away from the point. Because an exam can only last so long, the teacher should direct the student not to write everything he knows about the subject, but specifically to "compare the outcomes" or "give conclusions." These key words should be pointed out to the student prior to his writing so that he will write exactly what is wanted.

Most essay questions should receive an organized answer. Most students, however, start writing on the first idea that pops into their heads after reading a question, and then continue with whatever ideas come to mind next. The results are usually a weird sequence of ideas. The teacher who has a list of points which should be covered finds it difficult to determine how many points are included in such essays, and the result is a low grade. The students should be taught to organize their answers by jotting down a sketchy outline of key words that represent ideas to be included in the answer. The writing of the answer then becomes a matter of expounding on each of the ideas listed.

One common mistake made by students is to feel that a few words carry as much meaning to the teacher as they do to the student himself. Elaboration to show full understanding is different from "padding," which is readily recognized. Padding means bringing in irrelevant ideas or repeating points already made in order to fill up space. The student should be made aware that explaining what he means, giving illustrations, or showing the implications of his ideas is a different matter.

Simple mechanics in writing examinations may also affect the grade the student receives. Examinations written in ink or with a hard pencil in legible handwriting are more easily read than those hastily written with a soft pencil. Also, the student should be told to take a few minutes at the end to proofread his answer. An accidentally omitted "not" or some other words may affect his grade.

SCORING ESSAY EXAMINATIONS

The major criticism of the essay question is the lack of consistency in the scoring procedures. However, if the question is clearly stated and the problem defined, it is not difficult for the teacher to determine whether or not the student solved the problem. A question which is vague makes consistency in scoring almost impossible. Careful question construction is, therefore, the first requirement in scoring essay examinations.

Good scoring procedures are also important. The following guidelines are those that have been most frequently suggested for reducing subjectivity and avoiding bias in the scoring operation.

1. The first step is for the teacher to determine what constitutes a "good" answer. Will the organization of the answer be important? Will the amount of the factual knowledge applied to

the problem be judged an important factor? Will it be appropriate to categorize the acceptable responses to the question as "essential points" and "desirable points"? In other words, when each question is written, an outline of the number of points or ideas to be developed should be made, with the number of score points to be allotted each factor in arriving at a total question score. Allowances should be made for the possibility of creative students devising better answers than the teacher considered.

2. Score, if possible, without knowledge of the name of the student. This will eliminate the "halo" effect, and the papers will be graded on their own merit. If the identity of the student is known, the score assigned is often a reflection of the student's previous performance rather than his actual answer. You can have the student write his name on the last sheet of test papers and refrain from looking at it, or you can assign each student a number, thus eliminating to some extent the urge to look at the names.

3. Score the same question for all of the students at the same time. That is, score the first question for all before going to the second one. With this procedure, the teacher can get a "feel" for each question and enable himself to compare student answers. An efficient way of doing this is to have each question answered on a separate sheet of paper, with a student number on each, and pile each question separately. In this way the teacher can keep just one set of scoring criteria in his mind. This method tends to increase scoring efficiency, makes evaluative judgments easier, and reduces the total scoring time of the test.

4. If possible, score each set of answers without interruption. Unfortunately, part of the unreliability of scoring essay questions results from the feelings and attitudes of the teacher scoring the answers. This fluctuation of feeling may vary markedly throughout the day, or from day to day. Thus, you may not be as lenient if you are missing your favorite television program as you would be during the cartoon show that just preceded it.

5. Try not to permit your scoring to be influenced by irrelevant factors. If the scoring is to be valid, it must reflect the students' achievement of the specific objectives. If your objectives do not deal with handwriting, spelling, and/or neatness, then these factors should not influence the students' scores. If a teacher feels that these factors should be evaluated, then a separate score should be given, i.e., one evaluating the student's achievement of a specific objective, and another score evaluating the student's handwriting, spelling, and/or neatness.

SUMMARY STATEMENT

The construction and scoring of a good essay question requires time and effort. A good essay question measures student ability to propose, to select, and to organize ideas in writing, and consequently motivates the student to develop the ability to think and to write in his own words.

SUGGESTED READINGS

Ebel, R. L., *Measuring Educational Achievement*. Englewood Cliffs, N.J.: Prentice-Hall, Inc., 1965, Chap. 4. A good discussion concerning when to use essay questions. He offers suggestions on the construction and grading of them.

Godshalk, F. I., F. Swineford, and W. E. Coffman, *The Measurement of Writing Ability*. New York: College Entrance Examination Board, 1966. A booklet clearly written and well illustrated, indicating an approach for the measurement of writing ability.

Horrocks, J. E., *Assessment of Behavior*. Columbus, Ohio: Charles E. Merrill Books, Inc., 1964, pp. 470–473. A short critique concerning the essay question's weaknesses. Offers suggestions for improvements in the essay format if it is used in the school.

Lien, A. J., *Measurement and Evaluation of Learning*. Dubuque, Iowa: William C. Brown Company, Publishers, 1967, pp. 72–74. A basic discussion for the construction of essay questions.

Lindeman, R. H., *Educational Measurement*. Glenwood, Ill.: Scott, Foresman & Company, 1967, pp. 66–71. A presentation listing the advantages and scoring procedures for the essay question.

Lindvall, C. M., *Testing and Evaluation: An Introduction*. New York: Harcourt, Brace & World, Inc., 1961, Chap. 5. The nature of the essay question and its applicability to the measurement of educational objectives is discussed.

Noll, V. H., *Introduction to Educational Measurement*. Boston: Houghton Mifflin Company, 1965, pp. 131–137. A clear and concise discussion with illustrations covering the advantages of the essay question. Suggestions for improving this type of question are also listed.

Payne, D. A., *The Specification and Measurement of Learning Outcomes*. Waltham, Mass.: Blaisdell Publishing Company, 1968, Chap. 5. A comprehensive coverage of the construction and scoring of essay questions. It contains excellent illustrations as to methods of scoring essay questions.

6

Suggestions for Writing
Objective Questions

Most teachers use a wide variety of types of objective questions in their classroom examinations. This practice is illustrated by the following comment.

> I use just about every type depending on my time and the nature of the material that is being covered. I usually mix the types on my tests. (12th Grade, Social Studies Teacher)

As beginning teachers soon discover, the writing of many types of questions is not a simple task. There are no simple rules that can be followed to ensure a "good" question. The development of good questions requires a great deal of time, patience, and a thorough knowledge of the course content and specific objectives of the unit to be tested. A teacher can usually acquire the skills for constructing good objective questions over a period of time, but this is of little help to the new teacher confronted with the task of developing one of his first classroom tests.

SUGGESTIONS FOR WRITING OBJECTIVE QUESTIONS

Even though there is no "magic" formula to follow in the construction of good objective questions, there are some suggestions that may assist a teacher in writing questions and improving the reliability and validity of his tests.

1. *Format of the test page.* Don't clutter it up by trying to put

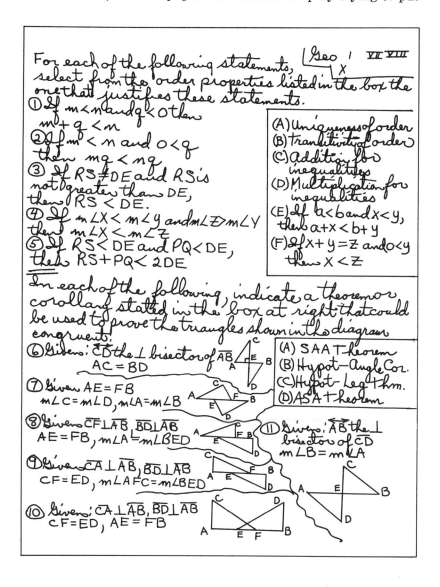

too many questions on one sheet. The figure shows an extreme example that was used in a geometry class.

A classroom test should be used to find out how much a student knows about the objectives of the course. If the ability to solve a maze is not an objective of this geometry class, then the validity of this test is questionable. The student confronted with this page could ask a number of questions, ranging from "Where do I put my name?" through "Where do I put the answers?" to "What do all those abbreviations mean?"

The directions for each sequence of questions should be clearly stated so that each student understands exactly what he is supposed to do. It is often good practice to state in the directions (as in the case of the first section of the example) that the properties listed in the box at the right may apply to more than one statement.

Needless to say, the questions should be spaced out, especially if the examination is handwritten, to make sure each student can read the statement without difficulty. Also, all parts of the question should be together in order for the student to face the task assigned. Looking at the "jigsaw" in the second part of the example, the students' task is complicated by the fact that the triangles are not below the "Given" part of the question, but squeezed in where they will fit. Nonstandard abbreviations should not be used on classroom exams.

2. *Test only the important material.* At times, irrelevant or incidental information appears in a teacher-made test. Each question should be checked to make sure that it includes only the material you consider important. In addition, try to make sure that you are not testing general experience, ability to read fast, background knowledge, or intelligence, when you want to test for knowledge of specific facts. The student should not be able to get a high score on a classroom test *merely* because he is bright.

3. *Aim at or below the reading level of the group you are testing.* Unless you are measuring language skills, the students' reading ability should not influence their responses to the questions. Ordinarily you want to use the simplest language possible to ensure complete understanding of the question.

4. *Use review and conference to make sure that each question is as foolproof as possible.* The right answer for each question should be selected by other informed individuals, rather than the incorrect choices. The old adage, "two heads are better than one," applies in this suggestion. No one person, however skillful, can foresee all of the possible meanings that others will see in a

question. If possible, it is well to have a fellow teacher review each of the test questions for ambiguity and clarity. If this is not possible, let the questions "cool off" for a few days and then take a second look for possible flaws. It is best never to use a question of which you are unsure; these are the ones that will certainly cause you and your students difficulty.

5. *Directions should be clear and complete.* Every series of questions should have directions that tell the students exactly what is expected of them. For example, on a multiple-choice test in which the students will record their answers on the exam paper, the following directions could be used:

> On the blank preceding each of the following questions, write *one* letter to indicate the correct, or best, answer.

Objective-type questions can be classified in a number of ways. One method is to divide them into two groups: those which demand recall, e.g., completion or identification; and those which call for recognition of the correct answer, e.g., true-false, matching or multiple-choice. Either type can be a good question if it is designed to measure those things the students have been studying.

For the purpose of this discussion, the objective-type questions have been classified under four main headings: (1) true-false; (2) multiple-choice; (3) matching; and (4) completion. The remaining sections of this chapter will discuss each of these main types and some of their modifications.

TRUE-FALSE QUESTIONS

The true-false format is very popular with teachers and is used quite often on teacher-made tests. Its popularity is based, to some extent, on the erroneous belief that this type of question is easy to write and score. In truth, the writing of a good true-false question requires almost as much time and effort as any other objective-type format.

Students have mixed emotions regarding the true-false questions on a classroom test. Some find them difficult to answer, while other feel that they are easier because of the possibility of guessing the right answer. Comments like the following are typical of the latter group's attitude concerning this format: "I'd rather take a true-false test than any other because they are easier. There are only two possible answers. You have a 50-50 chance."

There are three basic types of true-false questions. The *modified* type is built on a pattern of brief description of two things and their degree of relationship to each other; e.g., "Some high school students are unable to do any problems in simple multiplication of whole numbers." The two things in the statement are usually true, but are made false by changing the modifier so as to overstate or understate the degree of relationship. The following series of modifiers are typically used in classroom exams.[1]

All	Most	Some	No
Always	Usually	Sometimes	Never
Great	Much	Little	No
More	Equal	Less	
Positively related	Negatively related	Not related	
Good	Bad		
Is	Is not		

Teachers should realize that when a "test-wise" student sees one of these in a sentence, he can usually test whether the statement is true by substituting the other words (modifiers) in the series. If none of them make a better statement than the modifier already used, then the sentence is true. The above example, "Some high school students are unable to do any problems in simple multiplication of whole numbers," is tested by substituting as follows.

> All high school students are unable to do any problems in simple multiplication of whole numbers.

> Most high school students are unable to do any problems in simple multiplication of whole numbers.

> No high school students are unable to do any problems in simple multiplication of whole numbers.

In addition, most teachers have learned *not* to use "no," "never," "every," "all," or "entirely," because they usually cause the statement to be false. In other words, it is difficult to make any statement which is true of all or no items to which it refers.

The *unmodified* true-false question is usually a simple statement that may be either true or false. The student merely indicates whether or not a statement is true.

[1] F. P. Robinson, *Effective Study*, rev. ed. (New York: Harper & Row, Publishers, 1961), p. 58.

Directions: Some of the following statements are true and some are false. If the statement is true place a "T" in the blank space at the left. If the statement is false place an "F" in the space.

___(F)___   1. The ohm is the unit of current.

Directions: A series of questions is listed below. Each of them can be answered by "yes" or "no." Circle the correct answer at the left of the question.

(Yes) No 2. Is the presidential candidate who receives a majority of electoral votes elected president?

The *cluster* type true-false question is similar to the unmodified type. It usually consists of an incomplete statement followed by several phrases or clauses, each of which will complete the statement. The student is required to identify those phrases or clauses which form true statements and those which form false statements. The cluster true-false questions can be used to check several points concerning a particular concept or principle.

Directions: Each of the incomplete statements below is followed by several phrases, each of which completes the statement and makes it true or false. If the completed statement is true circle the "T" before the question. If false, circle the "F."

The major advantage of a frequency modulation (FM) signal for radio is that it

(T)   F   3. needs an antenna.
T   (F)   4. can be received on an AM radio set.
(T)   F   5. is relatively static free.
T   (F)   6. needs no carrier wave.

Advantages

1. The true-false item is generally used quite often and is therefore well known to most students. This is an advantage; students know how to answer this kind of question.
2. The true-false question can be used to test a wide range of subject matter because the questions can be answered quickly and a large number of them can be included on a single test. Generally, the average student is able to answer between three and five true-false questions in a minute. Naturally, the number

of questions answered will vary with the type of student and the type of material being tested.

3. The true-false question can be scored quickly and objectively.

4. The true-false item, and in fact any test question format, can be used to stimulate discussion and interest in a new assignment, or to locate points students have missed that must be retaught. This instructional use is often overlooked by the teacher.

Limitations

1. The true-false question tends to encourage the student to guess. In most true-false tests many of the questions can be answered without any knowledge of the subject matter involved.

2. It is difficult to construct a series of test questions that are either completely true or completely false without making the correct response "stand out."

3. This type of test is likely to be low in reliability unless it includes a large number of questions.

4. Many true-false tests include minor or irrelevant points which are given the same credit as significant points.

Suggestions for Constructing True-false Questions

A teacher can follow certain general suggestions in constructing adequate true-false examinations; however, none of these are foolproof.

1. Approximately half the questions should be true and half false. Students soon notice if you have the habit of making many more true statements than false ones. As a consequence, they are more apt to guess the correct answer. Whenever they do not know the answer they will mark it true, hoping that the law of averages will be on their side.

2. Randomize the pattern of correct responses. Try to ensure that the students will not be able to answer a question true simply because a certain number of false questions precede it, therefore making it time for a different response.

3. Make the method for indicating the correct answer as simple as possible. Most teacher-made tests have the student write in a letter or a code to indicate whether a statement is true or false. Others have the student circle the appropriate response. If you are going to have the student write in a letter or code, it

is better to use a $+$ and 0 rather than a $+$ and $-$. As an example, how would you grade the following responses:

$-$ 7. The garter snake is a reptile. ($+$ or $-$)
T 8. Sound travels faster in air than in solids. (T or F)

Although student responses such as these are sometimes planned and sometimes the result of carelessness, the student should be told that unless the answer is clearly marked, his answer will be wrong. In addition, it is better not to have the student write in the word true or false, as this takes unnecessary time and reduces the number of questions the student can answer.

Sample directions to use with true-false questions are included with the sample items in the preceding part of the chapter.

4. Avoid using statements directly from textbooks. This common fault in constructing true-false questions encourages the student to memorize statements without understanding what they mean. These "lifted" statements often do not convey the true meaning intended by the author, and as a result the students are confused and may mark them wrong even though they know the point being tested.

5. Use quantitative statements whenever possible. Quantitative language conveys to the student more exactly the meaning intended. Qualitative terms such as few, many, large, small, old, young, important, and unimportant are vague and indefinite to the student, and should be avoided.

(T) F 9. Benjamin Franklin lived a long time ago.
Better:
(T) F 9. Benjamin Franklin lived in the sixteenth century.

6. Use positive statements. Negative statements tend to be confusing to the student. Such questions place too great a premium on reading skill and knowledge of grammar. Unless this is an objective of your test, it is better to use positive statements.

T (F) 10. The true-false question is *not* a good format for measuring factual knowledge.
Better:
T (F) 10. The true-false question is a good format for measuring controversial material.

Take particular care to avoid double negatives. Such statements are particularly bad, since students knowledgeable in English grammar would recognize that two negatives are equal to an affirmative statement, while others would merely interpret such statements as emphatic negatives.

7. Avoid using trick statements, which are poor measures of student achievement. A student may know the point being measured but not be able to detect the "joker" that determines the correct answer. Trick or catch questions do not therefore, measure what the students know about the subject, but rather their level of intelligence or alertness. In the students' language, an example of a "dirty" question is:

    T   (F)   11.   The Bill of Rights was signed by Thomas Jeffersen.

Better:

    (T)   F   11.   The Bill of Rights was signed by Thomas Jefferson.

8. State in your directions whether you plan to correct for guessing, and also the method that you will use. To correct for guessing means that a student score on an exam is reduced in proportion to the number of wrong answers. This procedure is sometimes applied in scoring true-false or multiple-choice questions. When a teacher uses this method, he is attempting to discourage guessing and obtain a more accurate ranking of his students in terms of their true knowledge of the subject matter. There have been various formulas devised, but the most widely used is to subtract the number wrong from the number right. It is felt that teacher-made tests are not significantly improved by using a correction formula, but it is for each teacher to decide whether to correct for guessing when using true-false questions. Most teachers use a wide variety of objective formats in their exams and do not feel that a correction formula is necessary for the few true-false questions that are included.

MULTIPLE-CHOICE QUESTIONS

The multiple-choice format is usually considered the most useful and flexible of all objective-type question forms. It is used to measure student achievement of almost all teaching objectives in the schools. This format is as good as the true-false questions for measuring factual knowledge, but has the additional advantage of successful use in measuring such objectives as critical thinking, application of knowledge to unique situations, and understanding. Possibly the only kind of objective that this format does not measure satisfactorily involves the students' ability to organize material and write clearly. As indicated in Chapter 5, the essay question is perhaps the only satisfactory way of measuring achievement of such objectives.

The multiple-choice question consists of a question or incomplete statement followed by several possible answers, only one of which is correct or definitely better than the others. There are four basic forms of the multiple-choice question. The first, *right answer*, is the simplest kind. The student only has to identify the correct answer listed among others that are wrong, but not obviously wrong.

> *Directions:* Each of the questions or incomplete statements listed below is followed by several words, phrases, or series of numbers. From these, you are to choose the one which answers the question or completes the statement correctly. Place the letter of the word or phrase (A, B, C, or D) in the numbered blank space at the left of the question.
>
>   C   1. An injunction is a
>
>   A. part of speech.
>   B. union of two things.
>   C. court order.
>   D. form of advice.
>
>   B   2. Which one of the following is an example of citrus fruit?
>
>   A. Pear
>   B. Grapefruit
>   C. Pineapple
>   D. Apricot

The second variation of the multiple-choice format is the *best answer* form. Here the student selects the best answer from a series of several possible answers. This form is usually considered the most valuable of all the multiple-choice forms. In order for the student to identify the correct answer, varying amounts of judgment, inferential reasoning, or complete understanding of the subject are required. A major goal of most teaching is to get the students to the point at which they can make judgments, draw conclusions, and arrive at decisions. If these are important goals, then measurement of the students' progress toward these goals is important.

> *Directions*:   Each of the questions or incomplete statements listed below is followed by several possible answers. Choose the answer that *best* answers the question or completes the statement. Place the identifying letter of that answer (A, B, C, or D) in the numbered blank space at the left of the item.

D   3.   In the past strong third parties in American national politics have existed for only a short time because

    A.   they were too radical.
    B.   Congress legislated them out of existence.
    C.   the issues they raised disappeared with changing conditions.
    D.   the reforms they advocated were usually absorbed into the major party programs.

B   4.   Mrs. Brown's first child walked when he was 15 months old, so when her second child was that age, she gave him walking exercises. In spite of this exercise, however, the second child did not walk until he was 17 months old. This may be accounted for by the fact that

    A.   maturation depends on learning ability.
    B.   learning depends upon maturation.
    C.   conditioning depends upon learning ability.
    D.   the first child was advanced in its development.

The *association type* of multiple-choice question includes a word, phrase, or illustration followed by several choices, one of which is most closely associated with the first part.

Directions: In the following group of words, the first word is closely related to another word in the group. Select the word to which the first word is most closely related. Place the identifying letter of the word in the blank space at the left of the question.

C   5. Male germ cell:

      A. ovum
      B. zygote
      C. spermatozoon
      D. gamete

A   6. The degree of brightness of a color:

      A. intensity
      B. value
      C. strength
      D. energy

The fourth type, *analogy question,* requires the student to discover the relationship that exists between the first two parts of the question, and then apply this relationship to the third and fourth parts. The third part is given, but the fourth must be selected from several choices on the basis of the relationship existing between the first two parts.

Directions: In the following items determine the relationship between the first two parts of the question. Then apply this relationship to the third and fourth parts by selecting the proper choice (A, B, C, or D) to go with the third part. Place the letter of your choice in the blank space at the left of the question.

C   7. Electricity : Edison : : Telephone :   ?

      A. Franklin
      B. Caslon
      C. Bell
      D. Whitney

A   8. Hydro : Thermo : : Wet :   ?

      A. Warm
      B. Damp
      C. Power
      D. Shock

Advantages

1. The multiple-choice question can measure successfully a wide variety of instructional objectives.
2. Students are usually well acquainted with this format and it is not difficult for them to understand and use it.
3. The guessing factor does not present as great a problem with this format as with the true-false format.
4. Scoring may be entirely objective. It can be scored by hand or by machine.

Limitations

1. It is extremely difficult to construct a multiple-choice question that measures something more than factual knowledge.
2. The multiple-choice item is space-consuming. That is, fewer questions of this type will fit on a page.
3. It takes a relatively long time to construct good multiple-choice questions.
4. It is difficult to construct a question so that only one response is the correct one. Also, it is difficult to devise questions in which all of the possible responses are plausible and do not present clues that make the right answer obvious.
5. The multiple-choice question does not provide the student the opportunity for self-expression.

Suggestions for Constructing Multiple-choice Questions

1. Arrange the series of answers to each item in a vertical list. This not only helps the student see the task at hand, but also eases the revision of the first draft questions. In the examples given earlier, you should note that the answers are indented slightly in order to avoid momentary confusion with the last line of the question or incomplete statement.
2. Try to use more than three possible responses to each question. The best number of item answers is usually four or five. There is a rapid increase in item reliability from two to four answers, and only a slight increase between four and five.
3. Arrange the responses so that the correct one occurs in random order. Random order implies occasional repetition of correct answers with the same letter, but not more than three

correct answers with the same letter should appear in sequence.

4. All the responses should be equally plausible. The aim should be to make each suggested response so inviting as to tempt students who have only a superficial knowledge of the point involved. The plausibility of incorrect responses may be increased by using expressions very similar to those in the incomplete statement or the question.

5. All responses should be grammatically consistent with the question or the incomplete statement. For example, if the verb is plural, avoid singular responses. It is also good practice to avoid using "a" or "an" as the word in an incomplete statement preceding the list of responses.

<u>   B   </u>   9.   In the garage, there was an

      A.   rake.
      B.   oil can.
      C.   shovel.
      D.   car.

The use of the article "an" suggests that all but one of the responses can be eliminated, and hence the student is given a clue.

It should also be noted that the responses to the question-and-answer format begin with a capital letter, while in the incomplete statement format the answers begin with a small letter followed by a period.

6. The problem of the question should be put in the introductory statement or question, not in the answers. It is often possible to phrase the problem so completely in the introductory material that the answers consist of single words or phrases which don't sacrifice any of the complexity of the problem itself. This arrangement saves time and focuses the problem where you want it. It should be remembered that a multiple-choice question is not merely an incomplete statement followed by four or five true-false statements, only one of which is true. It is a test item in which the student's task is to choose the correct or best answer from several given answers or options.

7. The right answer should not be different in appearance from the other responses. The correct answer should be approximately the same length and at the same level of vocabulary as the distractors. A student may score higher than he should by merely selecting a response that is the longest, most carefully worded, or noticeably qualified.

MATCHING QUESTIONS

This type of question format requires the matching of two or more sets of materials in accordance with given directions. In its most commonly used form, it consists of two columns of words or phrases. The student is asked to match each item in one list with an item in the other list to which it is most closely related. The matching question, strictly speaking, is a variation of the multiple-choice format in which the same choices are applicable in answering each of the items. The following example will first be presented in a matching format and then, with slight modifications, two of the four possible multiple-choice items that could be made from this same material will be shown.

Directions: The two columns below contain related words and phrases pertaining to teacher-made tests. Select the type of teacher-made test format in the right-hand column that is most closely related to the descriptive phrase in the left-hand column, and place the identifying letter in the blank space provided by each question.

(B)	1. Its most common form is a simple declarative statement.	A. essay B. true-false C. short answer and completion D. multiple-choice E. matching
(A)	2. A test composed of this type of question usually has relatively few items in it.	
(C)	3. Items of this type are well suited to testing ability to solve numerical problems.	
(D)	4. This item consists of a problem whose answer must be identified in a series of possible answers.	

Here are multiple-choice questions derived from the preceding material.

(B)   1.   Which of the following teacher-made test formats is a simple declarative statement in its commonest form?

     A.   Essay
     B.   True-false
     C.   Short answer or completion
     D.   Multiple-choice
     E.   Matching

(C)   3.   Which of the following teacher-made test formats is well suited to testing ability to solve numerical problems?

     A.   Essay
     B.   True-false
     C.   Short answer or completion
     D.   Multiple-choice
     E.   Matching

The preceding item format has been found useful in cases in which a teacher wishes to test for knowledge of relationships between one set of objects (or persons, symbols, or places) and another.

There are numerous variations of the matching-type question. A few varieties illustrated in the following examples will give you an idea of the flexibility of this type of format. Keep in mind, however, that still other modifications can be made to suit your individual purposes.

Terms and Their Definitions

Directions: The two columns below contain terms and definitions relating to architecture. Match each definition in the left-hand column with the proper term in the right-hand column. Place the identifying letter of the term in the blank space provided by each question number.

(C)   5.   Principal front of a building   A. abutment

(B)   6.   A support against a lateral thrust of a building   B. buttress
                  C. facade
                  D. haunch
                  E. horse-shoe
                  F. impost

(G)   7.   An arch having both a concave and a convex curve   G. ogee
                  H. pier

(D)   8.   The place where an arch is weakest

Identification

Directions: The columns below contain illustrations of geometric figures and their names. You are to match the names in the left-hand column with the proper illustrations in the right-hand column. Place the identifying letter in the blank space provided by each name.

(G)	9. Right triangle	A.
(I)	10. Isosceles triangle	B.
(B)	11. Equilateral triangle	
(H)	13. Rhombus	C.
(C)	12. Rectangle	D.
		E.
		F.
		G.
		H.
		I.

Symbols and Their Names

Directions: The two columns below contain illustrations of electrical symbols and their proper names. You are to match each name in the left-hand column with the proper symbol in the right-hand column. Use each symbol only once.

(H)	14. Battery	A. ——×——
(F)	15. Resistance	B. —୦∿୦—
(D)	16. Antenna	C. —୦୦୦—
(B)	17. Fuse	
(C)	18. Inductance	D.
		E.
		F. —∿∿∿—
		G. —┤ ├—
		H. —┤╎╎╎╎├—

An often-used variation of the matching-type question is the key-list format. This type of question is preceded by a series of words or phrases to which succeeding items are to be related.

Directions: Which factors of a good test, reliability, validity, or objectivity, are implied or referred to in the statements below? In the blank before each statement place the letter of the term which you believe is implied or referred to by the speaker.

A. Reliability
B. Validity
C. Objectivity

(B) 19. "I wonder if this test will tell me what the students know of the subject?"

(A) 20. "Jim, you have taken this exam twice and you have missed the same questions each time."

(C) 21. "If you are going to help me correct the test, use the scoring key I made out, for the key is the only fair judge to all the students."

(A) 22. "Well, the test is finally finished and it contains questions from all levels of difficulty."

The number of questions that can be used with this type format is determined by the teacher. The above illustration contains just four of a possible eight or ten questions.

Advantages

1. The matching question is especially applicable for measuring the students' ability to recognize relationships and make associations, and for naming and identifying things learned. Micheels and Karnes have listed a number of areas for which the matching item format can be used.[2]

> The matching exercise may require the student to match such things as:
> a. Terms or words with their definitions
> b. Characteristics with the mechanical units to which they apply
> c. Short questions with their answers
> d. Symbols with their names
> e. Descriptive phrases with other phrases
> f. Causes with effects
> g. Parts or mechanical units with their proper names
> h. Principles with situations in which the principles apply
> i. Parts with the unit to which they belong
> j. Problems with their solutions

2. This type of item is relatively easy to construct. A large number of responses can be included in a small space, with one set of directions.

3. It is objective and can be scored quickly.

Limitations

1. One of the major limitations of this item format is that it is likely to contain irrelevant clues to the correct response.

2. It is likely to overemphasize the memorization of facts. Because this type of question is relatively easy to construct, the matching item is often used when another type of question format would provide a more valid measurement.

Suggestions for Constructing Matching Questions

1. Include only homogeneous material in each matching item. When unrelated materials are included, the correct response can

[2]W. J. Micheels and M. R. Karnes, *Measuring Educational Achievement* (New York: McGraw-Hill Book Company, 1960), p. 233.

usually be determined by the process of elimination. In the following example, although the responses are generally related to the game of tennis, some of them contain definitely unrelated material and should not be included in the question.

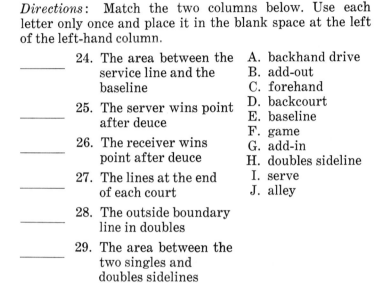

Directions: Match the two columns below. Use each letter only once and place it in the blank space at the left of the left-hand column.

_____ 24. The area between the service line and the baseline

_____ 25. The server wins point after deuce

_____ 26. The receiver wins point after deuce

_____ 27. The lines at the end of each court

_____ 28. The outside boundary line in doubles

_____ 29. The area between the two singles and doubles sidelines

A. backhand drive
B. add-out
C. forehand
D. backcourt
E. baseline
F. game
G. add-in
H. doubles sideline
I. serve
J. alley

A student considering this question could automatically eliminate four of the items in the right-hand column which are irrelevant to the questions, i.e., A, C, F, and I. This leaves six possible responses (which can be used only once) for six questions. Question 28 provides a clue, the "outside boundary line in doubles," and can quickly be matched up with H. Question 27 provides no difficulty for a student, as the answer E is the most logical. The same is true for question 24. Question 29 then must be J. Questions 25 and 26 are nothing more than true-false items. It would be easier to guess the right answer in this particular question than in a series of true-false statements covering the same material.

2. Include at least three extra choices from which responses will be chosen. This tends to reduce the possibility of guessing. If, for example, your directions state that a response can be used only once and you have five questions, you should have at least eight possible and plausible responses from which the student must select.

3. Have at least four and not more than twelve items in each matching question. There is no basis for these arbitrary limits other than common sense and experience. When there are fewer than four items, the material can usually be measured just as effectively with another type of format. When there are more than twelve items, this format tends to become confusing and the students waste time by having to search through too many possible choices.

4. Make the directions clear and very specific. Tell the students the area of instruction to which the two columns apply. Explain to them how the matching is to proceed and if the responses are to be used only once. The directions included in the earlier section will serve as useful guides.

COMPLETION QUESTIONS

For purposes of definition, the completion item is considered as that type where the student supplies the answer. The student may be required merely to supply a single word missing from a statement; he may answer a question by writing in a single word, figure, phrase, or date; or there may be a problem to complete, a list to enumerate, or a diagram to fill in.

The *simple completion* item usually requires the student to supply a word, figure, or date. The word (sometimes more than one) may come at the end of a statement, it may be an answer to a question, or it may be associated with another word or phrase.

> *Directions*: Each of the statements below contains a blank at or near the end of the statement. You are to supply the missing word. Write your word in the large blank space at the left of the question.
>
> (moist)   1. In general, the amphibia have a body covered by a thin, flexible, and usually _____ skin.
>
> (webbed)   2. Amphibia feet, when present, are often _____ to aid in swimming.
>
> (water)   3. The amphibia spend most of their larval life in the _____ .

Directions: Answer each of the following questions by writing in the correct answer in the blank space at the left.

(Alps)   4. What mountain range runs along the border between Italy and Switzerland?

(Tiber)   5. On what river is Rome located?

(Africa)   6. What continent lies to the south of Italy?

Directions: Listed below are several inventions. In the blank space before each invention write in the name of the inventor commonly associated with the invention.

(Bell)   7. Telephone

(Morse)   8. Telegraph

(Edison)   9. Phonograph

A second type of completion item is the *problem or situation* format. An ordinary arithmetic problem is an example of this item type. Variations can be devised to have the student do such things as complete a formula, fill in missing parts, or solve a problem using a specific formula. One example could be as follows.

Directions: Complete the following formulas by writing in the missing words, figures, terms, or symbols.

10. Circumference of a circle = ___(π r^2)___ .
11. The volume of a cylindrical tank is = ___(π r^{2}h)___ .
12. In the formula, v = v$_o$ + at, "a" represents ___(acceleration)___.

The third type of completion item, *identification*, may be used to measure the student's ability to indicate proper names for such things as symbols, drawings, tools, athletic equipment, or specific parts of insects.

Directions: Listed below are several symbols used by teachers in analyzing the students' scores on a teacher-made test. You are to write the proper meaning in the blank space at the left.

(mean)   13. M

(standard deviation)   14. S.D.

(median)   15. Md

Directions: You are to identify each of the parts of the tennis court indicated in the drawing below. Write the correct name in the blank space provided at the left.

(Right Service Court) _____ 16.

(Center Service Line) _____ 17.

(Center Service Mark) _____ 18.

(Service Line) _____ 19.

(Singles Sideline) _____ 20.

(Baseline) _____ 21.

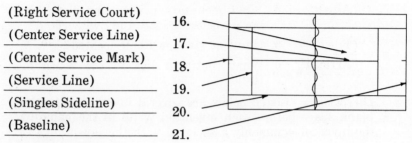

Advantages

1. The completion question can measure how much specific information a student knows, and is applicable to any subject area.

2. This format is relatively easy to construct. The most common types are used primarily in measuring "who," "what," "when," and "where" information.

3. The guessing factor is minimized in well prepared questions.

Limitations

1. Because this item type is easy to construct, teachers tend to use it excessively. As a result, there is an overemphasis of verbal facility and the memorization of facts.

2. Students may know the material but have difficulty in recalling the exact word to fill in a certain blank.

3. Unless care is taken in constructing this type of item, the scoring may become subjective. In other words, more than one word may be correct.

Suggestions for Constructing Completion Questions

1. Avoid indefinite statements.

_____ 22. Benjamin Franklin lived in _____.

This question does not tell the student whether the desired response is the date, the city, or the country. In other words, a legitimate response could be almost anything. The student should know exactly the type of response that is desired. Direct questions help in avoiding ambiguous statements and will result in a question that is easier to score.

2. Try to make completion questions as specific as possible. State the problem or describe the situation clearly by omitting only key words and not long phrases. Generally speaking, do not omit more than three words in a given sentence; a short statement with only one key word omitted is preferable.

3. Avoid taking statements directly from textbooks. This common fault of teachers constructing this type of item puts too great an emphasis on rote memorization.

4. In simple completion questions place the blank near or at the end of the statement. This practice allows the student to read through the question and then decide on the response. If the blank is put in the beginning, the student must read through the complete item and then mentally retrace his "steps" to decide what should be in the blank. An example will show the logic of this suggestion. This question was selected from a teacher-made test in Homemaking.

23. _____ wedding is characterized by a limited invitation list, one attendant, and modest decorations.

5. Try to construct the question so there is only one correct answer. This suggestion pertains primarily to the simple completion item, but is applicable to the other types. If synonyms are acceptable they should be identified before the exam and put on the answer key. This practice will avoid a number of arguments with students when the tests are returned.

6. Be sure there is plenty of room for the student to write in his responses. As you construct the items keep in mind the method that is to be used in scoring the questions. Whenever possible have all the spaces for responses on one side of the page, preferably the left-hand side. This makes for easier scoring. Most of the examples in the earlier section are arranged in this manner.

7. Keep the student in mind when you are constructing the questions. This format is more difficult than the other types of objective items and should be written in such a way that it will match the average student reading ability.

SUMMARY STATEMENT

The major advantages of objective-type questions are that they can be scored objectively and can cover a great deal of material in a limited amount of time. They must, however, be constructed with extreme care to make sure that they do not place too great an emphasis on memory for facts.

The true-false type items may be used where there are only two plausible alternative statements, and in situations where it is important to cover a number of concepts in a given period of time.

The most useful item type is the multiple-choice question. It can be used to test a number of different instructional objectives. If it is constructed carefully with at least four plausible alternatives, it will not provide too much opportunity for guessing.

The matching exercise provides an efficient way of testing certain types of associations. However, only homogeneous material should be included in each matching item.

Completion questions attempt to measure how much a student knows of specific information. It is a relatively easy format to construct and the guessing factor is minimized in well prepared questions.

SUGGESTED READINGS

Ahmann, J. S., and M. D. Glock, *Evaluating Pupil Growth.* Boston: Allyn & Bacon, Inc., 1967, Chaps. 3 and 4. These two chapters deal with the role of objective items in teacher-made tests.

Anastasi, A., ed., *Testing Problems in Perspective.* Washington, D.C.: American Council on Education, 1966.

Bloom, B. S., *et al., Taxonomy of Educational Objectives: Handbook I: Cognitive Domain.* New York: David McKay Co., Inc., 1956. Contains numerous illustrative items for each category in the taxonomy.

Diederich, P. B., "Exercise Writing in the Field of the Humanities," in A. Anastasi, ed., *Testing Problems in Perspective.* Washington, D.C.: American Council on Education, 1966, pp. 131–139.

Ebel, R. L., *Measuring Educational Achievement.* Englewood Cliffs, N.J.: Prentice-Hall, Inc., 1965, Chaps. 5 and 6. Discusses the construction of true-false and multiple-choice items. Numerous faulty true-false and multiple-choice test questions are shown and criticized.

Englehart, M. C., "Exercise Writing in the Social Sciences," in A. Anastasi, ed., *Testing Problems in Perspective.* Washington, D.C.: American Council on Education, 1966, pp. 153–164.

Gorow, F. F., *Better Classroom Testing.* San Francisco: Chandler Publishing Company, 1966, Chaps. 5, 6, 7. An excellent discussion with numerous illustrations showing how objective-type questions can be used to measure a broad range of instructional objectives.

Gronlund, N. E., *Constructing Achievement Tests.* Englewood Cliffs, N.J.: Prentice-Hall, Inc., 1968, Chaps. 3 and 4. A discussion showing how objective-type items can be used to measure knowledge and complex achievement areas.

Nedlsky, L., "Exercise Writing in the Natural Sciences," in A. Anastasi, ed., *Testing Problems in Perspective.* Washington, D.C.: American Council on Education, 1966, pp. 140–152.

Storey, A. G., "A Review of Evidence or the Case Against True-False Items," *Journal of Educational Research,* 1966, pp. 282–285. The advantages and limitations of this type item are evaluated. Five major points are presented for restricting the use of this type item.

Wood, D. A., *Test Construction, Development and Interpretation of Achievement Tests.* Columbus, Ohio: Charles E. Merrill Books, Inc., 1960, Chaps. 5, 6, 7. These three chapters are concerned with the preparation of objective test items.

7

An Objective Test:
Putting It Together
and Analyzing It

Developing an objective test is hard work. It starts with making a test plan, continues with the writing of questions, and finishes with the assembly of the questions and duplication of copies of the test. It is unfortunate that many teachers tend to overlook the "assembly" part in the construction of a test. It is in this phase that the teacher should answer the following questions:

1. In what order, or sequence, should the questions appear on the test?
2. Is my scoring key prepared?
3. Are my directions easily understood, complete, and to the point?
4. Is my test format confusing because it has too many questions on one sheet?
5. If I am going to use an answer sheet, is it prepared properly?

The Order of Questions   Teachers generally use a wide variety of objective questions on their tests. Some teachers will group their questions on the test according to the type of question format. That is, there will be separate sections for the true-false items, the multiple-choice, the completions, and the matching questions. Other teachers feel that mixing the different formats is a better way. There is not any one commonly agreed upon way for the ordering of the questions.

Some test experts suggest that the items be presented in order of difficulty, with the easy ones first and the hard questions last. This arrangement is virtually impossible if you have no record of past performance of students on each item.

One method that has worked quite well is to group the questions on the test in regard to the objectives they are measuring. In Chapter 4, four objectives were identified, i.e., knowledge of important terminology, knowledge of specific facts, knowledge of sequences or trends, and knowledge of the impact of slavery on the population of modern Brazil. Grouping the questions starting with terminology, followed by specific facts, then sequences and trends, and finally the impact of slavery on modern Brazil, would present a logical order of items, which is one of the ways to help students give their best performance on a test. It is also a check for you to see if you have sufficient questions to measure each objective.

Preparing the Scoring Key   The list of correct answers should be prepared at this stage instead of after the duplicating process. If the correct answers to objective items are to be in random order on the exam, the scoring key must be prepared at this time. This will give you the opportunity to shift the order of distractors in multiple-choice items in order to make them random in their sequence. Also, the true-false questions can be shifted so that no response pattern is evident to the student.

Directions   Clear directions are most important. The student should not have to spend a lot of time trying to figure out what he is expected to do. "Do I choose the best answer or the correct answer?" "Can I use the same answer twice in matching questions?" "Where do I do the computations necessary for this question?" "Should I guess if I don't know the answer?" "Can I mark the questions I don't know on the exam paper so I can go back and try and figure them out?" "Where do I put my answers?"

These are the types of questions that should be anticipated by the teacher. Clear directions simply stated in understandable words save the students' time and reduce confusion caused by questions asked during the exam. Chapter 6 showed different illustrations of directions for the different item formats which could be used as examples of good directions.

Test Format   Trying to put too many test questions on one sheet of paper is a common criticism of teacher-made tests. Look at the following example from a tenth-grade examination in World History.

_____ 1. The two privileged classes in France before the Revolution were the: (A) nobility and peasants, (B) nobility and clergy, (C) nobility and bourgeoisie, (D) clergy and bourgeoisie.

_____ 2. The members of the radical group that controlled the government during the latter part of the Revolution were called: (A) emigres, (B) Loyalists, (C) Jacobins, (D) monarchists.

_____ 3. The class that benefited most from the Revolution was the: (A) clergy, (B) nobility, (C) peasants, (D) bourgeoisie.

The ease of reading is improved by modifying the format of these questions.

_____ 1. The two privileged classes in France before the Revolution were the

A. nobility and peasants.
B. nobility and clergy.
C. nobility and bourgeoisie.
D. clergy and bourgeoisie.

This change in format does require more space, but it reduces greatly the confusion students face when the questions and the possible responses are bunched together. A test should not be a test of reading or ability to figure out a maze.

Answer Sheets   One of the most efficient methods for scoring objective classroom tests calls for a separate answer sheet, usually designed by the teacher. This answer sheet may be duplicated by any method, e.g., ditto, mimeograph, or printing, and can be used whenever an examination is given. A typical example of the form is shown in part. Notice that the letters on the answer sheet run in a sequence. For question number one, the possible alternative answers are lettered A, B, C, D, and E. Question number two has F, G, H, I, and J as possible alternative answers. Question three reverts back to the same sequence used by question one. This method reduces the possibility of the student losing his place when transferring his answer, and is less confusing for him.

Name _____

Date _____   Score _____

Period _____

READ THE DIRECTIONS ON THE TEST PAPER. MARK ALL AN-
SWERS ON THIS PAPER BY DARKENING THE LETTER WHICH
CORRESPONDS TO THE BEST ANSWER. USE PENCIL SO THAT YOU
CAN CHANGE YOUR ANSWER IF NECESSARY.

Item						Item					
1.	A	B	C	D	E	25.	A	B	C	D	E
2.	F	G	H	I	J	26.	F	G	H	I	J
3.	A	B	C	D	E	27.	A	B	C	D	E
.						.					
.						.					
.						.					
24.	F	G	H	I	J	50.	F	G	H	I	J

Section of a Teacher-designed Answer Sheet.

The scoring stencil for an answer sheet of this type can be made from a manila filing folder by aligning the stencil to match the answer sheet. Punch holes in the scoring stencil so that only the correct answers show when you place the stencil over a marked answer sheet.

Many teachers feel that the use of an answer sheet restricts them with regard to the number of different objective-type questions that they are able to use on their exams. Some teachers have devised answer sheets that can be used with several different types of objective items, usually grouped according to type and each group numbered independently. The way the student uses the answer sheet is described in the directions provided. Following is an illustration of a section of this type of answer sheet. Notice that the completion and matching sections are placed at the edges of the answer sheet to facilitate scoring by the teacher.

Name _____	Scores: Part A _____
	Part B _____
Period _____	Part C _____
	Part D _____
Date _____	Total _____

READ THE DIRECTIONS ON THE TEST PAPER. MARK ALL AN-SWERS ON THIS PAPER BY FILLING IN THE SPACE OR BY DARK-ENING THE LETTER WHICH CORRESPONDS TO THE BEST AN-SWER. USE A PENCIL SO THAT YOU CAN CHANGE YOUR ANSWER IF NECESSARY.

A: Completion		B: True-False		C: Multiple-Choice		D: Matching	
Item	Answer	Item	Answer	Item	Answer	Item	Answer
1.	_____	1.	T F	1.	A B C D E	1.	_____
2.	_____	2.	T F	2.	F G H I J	2.	_____
3.	_____	3.	T F	3.	A B C D E	3.	_____
4.	_____	4.	T F	4.	F G H I J	4.	_____

Section of a Teacher-designed Answer Sheet.

If you are not going to use an answer sheet, have a column of answer spaces on either the left-hand or right-hand side of the exam paper. This will reduce the amount of time needed to score the test. A "strip key" can be placed directly alongside the answer column. This key can be unused exam paper on which the correct answers have been written. The strip key can also be used when students write in their answers on a separate answer sheet.

ANALYSIS OF QUESTIONS

Generally speaking, most teachers consider a question good if students don't argue with them about the answer or if their students don't all get it right or wrong.

I try to find out why certain items are too hard. I drop the easy questions. (10th Grade, Geometry)

When going over it, sometimes I will detect that the question is poorly written because quite a number of students misunderstood it. Also if a number of students complain. (8th Grade, English)

I really don't have a good method. (12th Grade, Architectural Drawing)

A more scientific approach to this whole area, which greatly improves the quality of measuring student achievement, is through the use of item analysis data in the revision of tests and test questions. This assumes, however, that the test items were originally written carefully and cover materials that are not only important but also relevant to your specific objectives. No technique can compensate for lack of skill in item writing.

Three kinds of important information about the test and the quality of the questions can be obtained through item analysis. These are item difficulty, item validity, and effectiveness of distractors.

Item Difficulty   The usual purpose of an item difficulty index is to make it possible to know how many (or what percentage of) students will get the question right the next time it is used. Of course, this assumes that the next group of students who take the test will have been taught the same content with the same emphasis and are relatively similar, e.g., in age and ability, to the first group.

The easiest way to estimate the difficulty of an item is to use the following procedures.

1. Select the highest 27 per cent and the lowest 27 per cent of the test papers. If 27 per cent does not give you a whole number, take the number of papers above or below 27 per cent necessary to get one. Make sure, however, that you have an equal number of papers in both the high and low groups.
2. Count the number of correct answers to a particular question in both of these groups.
3. Divide the number of correct answers by the number of papers in both groups.

This will give a percentage figure or decimal which serves as the index of item difficulty. This index is the reverse of what you might expect, i.e., the larger the index number, the easier the question. In other words, a question so easy that every one gets it right (100 per cent) would have a difficulty index of 1.0, and an item so difficult that no one answered it correctly (0 per cent) would have an index of 0.0. Most questions on teacher-made tests fall somewhere between these two extremes.

Since the major purpose of a classroom exam is to discriminate among how much each student learned in a unit of instruction, it is desirable to have a test that yields a wide range of scores. Do not hesitate to include a couple of 1.0 items for student morale, but keep away from questions that no students can answer. With a multiple-choice test, the widest range of scores will usually result from a test whose average difficulty is around .5 or .6.

Item Validity   If a question is missed by all the students who did poorly on the exam (lower 27 per cent) and answered correctly by all the students who did well on the exam (upper 27 per cent), the item has perfect validity. In other words, item validity indicates the relative differences between the two groups in answering a certain question. Very seldom are perfectly valid questions found on any test. They usually fall somewhere along a continuum running from no validity (0.00) to highly valid (+1.00). If an item is found to have negative validity in any degree, it should be thrown out, as this item is penalizing the better student to the advantage of the poorer student.

Item validity may be computed by the following procedures.

1. Select the highest 27 per cent and the lowest 27 per cent of the papers. If 27 per cent does not give you a whole number, take the number of papers below or above 27 per cent necessary to get one. Make sure you have equal numbers of papers in both the high and the low group.
2. For each question, count the number of correct answers in the high group and in the low group.
3. Subtract the number of correct answers in the low group from the number in the high group.
4. Divide this difference by the number of papers in either group.

For example, the total number of papers we have is 150. Twenty-seven per cent of the 150 is approximately 40 papers, so the 40 highest scoring and the 40 lowest scoring papers are taken for analysis. If, for a given item, 30 students answered the question correctly in the high group and 10 selected the right answer in the low group, the computation is as follows:

$$\frac{30 - 10}{40} = .50 \quad \text{(validity index)}$$

This represents a satisfactorily high validity index for a teacher-made test, since it does indicate differences between the two groups of students. The item does, however, present some problems even for the students who did well on the exam.

A word of caution should be stated. The interpretation of a validity index of .50 does not mean that the question is 50 per cent valid. It simply means that this item is more valid than an item with a lower index. The index of validity is at best a rough estimate for determining whether a question discriminates between students who score high on a test and those who do not.

Effectiveness of Distractors   A multiple-choice question is only as good as its distractors. If two distractors in a four-choice item are completely implausible, the question is in effect a two-choice item and is made easier. It is, therefore, important for a teacher in improving his test questions to know the extent to which students who did well on the test and students who did poorly have selected the various distractors. A graphic method is to enter in

Course: General Math			Objective:		Multiplication of Percentage					
Question:	How much is 110% of 20?									
	A.	11								
	B.	22 (keyed)								
	C.	30								
	D.	42								
	E.	44								

Adminis- tered	Group	Distractors A	B	C	D	E	Omit	Total	Diff.	Valid	No.
1. 7/68	U	5	(30)	3	0	2	0	40	.5	.5	150
	L	8	(10)	15	0	7	0	40			
2.	U										
	L										

An Example of a Record-keeping Card for Multiple-choice Questions.

a table the number of students in the high group (upper 27 per cent) and the low group (lower 27 per cent) who chose each distractor.

A quick inspection of the example shows that distractor D is so implausible that it does not attract any member of the two groups and is in need of revision. The correct answer, B, separates the highs from the lows adequately, as do distractors C and E. Distractor A should be looked at, as it is not discriminating very well between the two groups.

SUMMARY STATEMENT

After a group of objective items have been written, they must be inspected and edited prior to being organized in a classroom examination. This process involves checking the relationship between each item and the test plan, removing any ambiguity or irrelevant clues that may still remain, establishing relative difficulty, and correcting any feature that negatively influences the students' understanding.

Organizing the objective items into an exam is a very important task. The arrangement of the questions on the test must be determined, either based upon the type of item or by a logical arrangement by the subject matter being tested. The length of the test must be determined. In addition, directions must be written and the scoring key prepared.

The analysis of the test questions after the test has been given is also important. The use of item analysis data in the revision of test questions greatly improves the quality of measuring student achievement.

SUGGESTED READINGS

Diederich, P. B., *Short-cut Statistics for Teacher-Made Tests*, Evaluation and Advisory Service Series, No. 5. Princeton, N.J.: Educational Testing Service, 1960.

Ebel, R. L., *Measuring Educational Achievement*. Englewood Cliffs, N.J.: Prentice-Hall, Inc., 1965, Chap. 11. This chapter outlines techniques of item analysis that are especially pertinent to the classroom teacher.

Gronlund, N. E., *Constructing Achievement Tests*. Englewood Cliffs, N.J.: Prentice-Hall, Inc., 1968, Chap. 6. Presents a list of guidelines to aid teachers in assembling, administering, and evaluating classroom tests.

Kelly, T. L., "The Selection of Upper and Lower Groups for the Validation of Test Items," *Journal of Educational Psychology*, 30 (1939), 17–24. This article presents the rationale for the selection of the upper and lower groups for the validation of test items.

Lindquist, E. F., ed., *Educational Measurement*. Washington, D.C.: American Council on Education, 1951, Chaps. 6 and 11. Chapter 6 is a comprehensive review of the problems and techniques for planning objective tests. Chapter 11 provides useful assistance in reproducing objective tests.

Travers, R. M. W., *How to Make Achievement Tests*. New York: The Odyssey Press, Inc., 1950. A practical handbook for teachers on the preparation of tests for classroom use. It includes suggestions on the assembly, administration, and scoring of objective tests, and a discussion of the significance of test scores.

8

The Mystery Hour:

A Few Statistics

Once the classroom exam has been constructed, administered, and scored, the teacher is faced with the task of making some sense out of all the scores and summarizing the results for both the students and his grade book. Teachers use a wide variety of methods of interpreting the scores and reporting the results to their students.

> I usually put a curve on the board. Tell them the average score. (11th Grade, U.S. History)

> They are given the number right. I then put the range on the board from the top grade to the lowest grade and indicate the percentiles and the cut-off points for specific grades. (12th Grade, Social Studies)

> First I get the number right and number wrong on a raw score basis. I do a frequency distribution and find the mean and the mode. Also, I give a letter grade. (11th Grade, U.S. History)

What do all these psychometric terms mean? The average score? Percentiles? The range? A frequency distribution? The mode? If they are being used by teachers, they must be serving some useful purpose. This chapter will discuss the statistics that are most useful to the classroom teacher in interpreting and summarizing the results of his tests. These procedures are presented in terms of the kinds of problem situations with which you are likely to be presented.

FREQUENCY DISTRIBUTIONS

Suppose a social studies teacher has given his class of 18 students an exam that has 50 objective questions, each worth one point. The number of points assigned to each student in the class record book is the number of right answers (see Table 8–1).

Looking at the list of scores in the record book, notice how hard it is to find any meaning for the numbers. With some effort, Janet can be identified as getting the highest score and Larry the lowest score. However, if you wanted to find out how many of the class scored above 35, or how many scored 32 points on the test, this would be rather difficult with such a list.

These characteristics of a class performance can be more easily determined if the scores are arranged in a frequency dis-

TABLE 8–1

Class Record Book

3rd Period	Social Studies	Mr. Sanders
Student	Exam: Brazil	
James	38	
Janet	44	
Paulita	34	
Larry	24	
Lynn	35	
George	42	
Elena	34	
Carl	40	
Carol	29	
Sidney	34	
John	32	
Elaine	33	
Mike	40	
Gloria	39	
Tony	29	
Tom	32	
Bob	43	
Lori	37	

tribution. The frequency distribution is merely a list of all scores, starting at the top with the highest and going down to the lowest, together with the number of times (frequency) that a score occurs (see Table 8–2).

TABLE 8–2

Distribution of Social Studies Exam Scores

Score	Tally	Frequency
44	1	1
43	1	1
42	1	1
41		0
40	\ 11	2
39	1	1
38	1	1
37	1	1
36		0
35	1	1
34	111	3
33	1	1
32	11	2
31		0
30		0
29	11	2
28		0
27		0
26		0
25		0
24	1	1

From these scores, Mr. Sanders may desire to make either or both of two types of descriptive statements. The first would involve a comparison of a student's score with the performance of the class as a whole. The other statement would involve a description of the performance of the entire class, i.e., statements about the distribution of the scores. Both of these require the determination of certain characteristics of the distribution which will be illustrated in the remaining sections of this chapter.

MEASURES OF CENTRAL TENDENCY

One of the main tasks of statistics is to reduce data into understandable terms. If, for example, Mr. Sanders wants to know how his class performed as a group on his classroom test, he would use certain methods to determine where all the students' scores are concentrated. These methods are usually called measures of central tendency and include the mean, the median, and the mode.

Mean   The mean is commonly referred to as the arithmetic average of all the test scores. It is obtained by adding all of the scores on the test and dividing this number by the number of scores (or students who took the test). Looking at Mr. Sanders' class in Table 8–1, the mean of the test scores is 35.5, as shown in Table 8–3. This figure points out that the mean is a number and not always an exact score, but it does tell Mr. Sanders the typical performance on the test by the whole class.

The mean can also be used to indicate how well a certain student did on the classroom exam. In other words, did he score above the mean or below it, and how far? It is good practice to include on the student's paper not only his raw score (the number of correct answers), but how far his score deviates from

TABLE 8–3

Calculation of the Mean

Student	Score	
Janet	44	
Bob	43	$M = \dfrac{\Sigma X}{N}$
George	42	
Carl	40	
Mike	40	
Gloria	39	$= \dfrac{639}{18}$
James	38	
Lori	37	
Lynn	35	$= 35.5$
Paulita	34	
Elena	34	
Sidney	34	
Elaine	33	N = number of scores
John	32	X = individual's
Tom	32	test score
Carol	29	
Tony	29	
Larry	24	
$N = 18$	$\Sigma X = 639$	

the mean. The following formula is used to determine the deviation value:

$$d = X - M$$

$$\text{where} \quad \begin{array}{l} d = \text{student's deviation score} \\ X = \text{student's test score} \\ M = \text{the mean of all the test scores} \end{array}$$

This simply states that a student's deviation score (d) is obtained by subtracting the mean (M) score of the distribution from the student's test score (X). Looking back at Table 8–1, Carl has a deviation score of +4.5.

$$d = X - M$$
$$= 40 - 35.5$$
$$= +4.5$$

Tony has a deviation score of −6.5.

$$d = X - M$$
$$= 29 - 35.5$$
$$= -6.5$$

Median   The median is defined as a point on a ranked distribution of test scores that neither exceeds nor is exceeded by more than half of the test scores. In other words, the median score of a ranked group of test scores is the central point of the distribution.

The median can be obtained easily if the set of scores is ranked from high to low. The procedure is the same if the number of test scores is an odd or even number. The only difference is that, when working with an odd number of test scores, the median will correspond to an actual score, whereas if the number of test scores are even, the median becomes a point in the distribution. In either case, the median satisfies its definition as the central point in the distribution.

The median can be computed easily if the set of scores are arranged according to magnitude and listed independently, as in Table 8–4. You will note that all of the scores are listed even though there is duplication of some of the magnitudes, e.g., 29, 32, 34, and 40. If, however, the scores are grouped in any way, the following formula is inappropriate.

In Table 8–4, 18 scores are listed. Using the following formula:

$$\frac{N + 1}{2} = \frac{18 + 1}{2} = 9.5$$

the median for this set of scores is determined by counting up from the bottom 9.5 scores. In this example, 9.5 scores from the

TABLE 8–4

Calculation of the Median

Score (X)	
44	
43	
42	$\text{Median} = \dfrac{N + 1}{2}$
40	
40	
39	$= \dfrac{18 + 1}{2}$
38	
37	
35	
34	$= 9.5 \quad (9.5 \text{ scores from}$
34	$\text{bottom})$
34	
33	$\text{Median} = 34.5$
32	
32	
29	
29	
24	
N = 18	

bottom is 34.5 and this is the median for this distribution of scores.

Mode   The mode is the score made most frequently by the students in the class. A glance at Mr. Sanders' class frequency distribution (Table 8–2) shows that a score of 34 is the most frequent score and is, therefore, the mode of the distribution. The mode is the most easily obtained measure of central tendency, but it is not as valuable in future analysis of data as the mean or the median. The chief value of the mode is that it is easily obtained by inspection and is useful in locating points of concentration of the same scores in a frequency distribution.

These three measures of central tendency give us information about the distribution of test scores. Each of these measures is used for different purposes, and the values of each are affected by the nature of the distribution. Some suggestions follow which will guide you in selecting one measure in preference to the other two.

1. Compute the arithmetic mean when:
   a. the greatest consistency of score value is wanted. The

mean will usually vary less from one distribution of test scores to another if both distributions are from the same or similar groups. For example, Mr. Sanders administered the same test to his three college-prep classes in social studies. If he wanted to compare the total performance of each of these classes, he would compute a mean.

b. you will be doing additional computations, such as finding the standard deviation of your classroom scores.

c. the distribution of scores approaches the shape and characteristics of the normal distribution curve. That is, when the scores or measures are distributed symmetrically about the mean, with as many cases at various distances above the mean as are at equal distances below the mean, and with cases concentrated near the average and decreasing in frequency the farther one departs from the average.

2. Compute the median when:

a. the distribution of scores *does not* approach the shape of the normal distribution curve. Sometimes the scores tend to group themselves more heavily toward one end of the distribution than the other. When this happens in a distribution, the scores are said to be skewed. Skew-

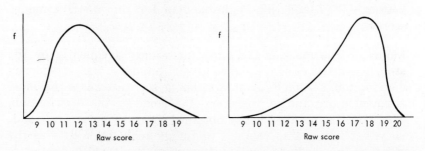

ness may indicate that a test is too easy or too difficult for the particular group being tested. A test that is too difficult would yield more low scores than is usual. The median, therefore, will give a truer picture of the typical performance of a group of students when the distribution is skewed.

b. you are interested in finding out whether the scores fall within the upper or lower halves of the distribution, but not particularly where they are in relation to the central point.

3. Compute the mode when:

a. a very rough estimate of a central value is needed.

b. you want to determine what is the most typical score in your class.

c. a quick estimate of a central value is wanted.

PERCENTILE SCORES

"How did I do on the test compared to the other members of the class?" "How many scored below me on the test?" These are typical questions often heard when a classroom test is handed back. Students are generally interested in how they did on the test in relationship to what the others in the class did. Percentile scores give you this information. The percentile score is the per cent of scores in a distribution equal to or lower than the score corresponding to a given score. In the preceding section, the median was defined as that point in a score distribution below which 50 per cent of the scores fall. The median is, therefore, the fiftieth percentile.

It is possible to calculate points on the distribution below which 25 per cent, 75 per cent, 84 per cent, or any per cent of the scores fall. These points are called percentiles and are commonly identified by the symbol P_n, where P is a percentile and n is the per cent of scores below a given value. The twenty-fifth percentile would be identified as P_{25}. The median would be P_{50}. P_{50} is read, for example, as the point below which 50 per cent of the scores fall. P_{25} is the point below which 25 per cent of the scores fall.

The general formula for finding P_n in a frequency distribution is:

$$P_n = p\% \ (N + 1) \ \text{score from the bottom}$$

For example, using the frequency distribution of Mr. Sanders' Social Studies class (Table 8–2), P_{75}, P_{25}, and P_{50} can be identified as in Table 8–5.

This method of calculating percentile scores should only be used when the scores are not grouped together. Each score should be separate, as in the example on p. 94.

MEASURES OF VARIABILITY

Most teachers are satisfied to stay with measures of central tendency and percentiles when trying to make sense out of their

TABLE 8–5
Calculation of Percentiles

Student	Score (X)	
Janet	44	
Bob	43	
George	42	$P_{25} = 25\% \ (N + 1)$
Carl	40	$= .25 \ (19)$
Mike	40	$= 4.75$ scores from bottom
Gloria	39	$= 32$
James	38	
Lori	37	$P_{50} = 50\% \ (N + 1)$
Lynn	35	$= .50 \ (19)$
Paulita	34	$= 9.5$ scores from bottom
Elena	34	$= 34.5$
Sidney	34	
Elaine	33	$P_{75} = 75\% \ (N + 1)$
John	32	$= .75 \ (19)$
Tom	32	$= 14.25$ scores from bottom
Carol	29	$= 40$
Tony	29	
~~Larry~~	~~24~~	

$N = 18$

students' performance on a classroom test. Their discomfort level rises when the concept of the standard deviation is introduced. The major reason they give is that they can see no relevance for its use in the analysis of test results. The point of this section is, therefore, an attempt to show you its importance.

Looking back at the scores the students earned on the social studies test, you notice that not everybody made the same score. Some students made scores above the mean while others were below the mean. These fluctuations of scores around the mean are called measures of variability or dispersion. Measures of this type are commonly used when we want to compare two or more sets of scores. For example, you may find that, on administering the same test to two comparable classes, they have exactly the same means and medians, and yet the distribution of scores in each class are very dissimilar.

You will notice in Table 8–6 that both classes have the same means and medians, but in Class A the scores tend to spread out considerably more than in Class B, whose scores tend to cluster around the mean.

These two groups of students differ from each other in their degree of variability (the fluctuation of scores) about the mean of the distribution. Therefore, some suitable measure of vari-

TABLE 8–6

Two Distributions with the Same Means and Medians but
Different Variabilities

Class A Scores (X)		Class B Scores (X)	
15		13	
13		12	
13		10	
10	Mean = 9	10	Mean = 9
9	Median = 8.5	9	Median = 8.5
8		8	
6		8	
6		7	
5		7	
5		6	
Σ X = 90		Σ X = 90	

ability in addition to a measure of central tendency is needed
to describe the two sets of test scores adequately. The two most
useful measures of variability for classroom teachers are range
and standard deviation.

Range   The range is the distance between the highest score
of the distribution and the lowest score. The range shows the
limit within which all of the test scores fall. For example, if the
highest score of a distribution is 15 and the lowest is 5, the range
is $15 - 5 = 10$. The larger the range, the greater the dispersion of scores from the mean value. Although the range is a good
preliminary procedure for determining this dispersion, it does
not indicate its pattern. A measure that will give this pattern
of dispersion is the standard deviation.

Standard Deviation   The standard deviation measures how
much the scores in a distribution are spread out or the amount
of their dispersion from the mean value. This measure is dependent upon the position of every score in the distribution, and the
computation is based on the deviation of each of the scores from
the mean. The formula for finding the standard deviation is:

$$S.D. = \sqrt{\frac{\Sigma d^2}{N}}$$
where

S.D. = the standard deviation
Σ d² = the sum of all squared deviations from the mean
N = the number of test scores

TABLE 8–7

Calculation of the Standard Deviation for Two Classes, Each with Ten Students and a Mean of Nine

Class A			Class B		
Score (X)	d	d²	Score (X)	d	d²
15	6	36	13	4	16
13	4	16	12	3	9
13	4	16	10	1	1
10	1	1	10	1	1
9	0	0	9	0	0
8	−1	1	8	−1	1
6	−3	9	8	−1	1
6	−3	9	7	−2	4
5	−4	16	7	−2	4
5	−4	16	6	−3	9
$\Sigma X = 90$	$\Sigma d = 0$	$\Sigma d^2 = 120$	$\Sigma X = 90$	$\Sigma d = 0$	$\Sigma d^2 = 46$

$$\text{S.D.} = \sqrt{\frac{\Sigma\ d^2}{N}} \qquad\qquad \text{S.D.} = \sqrt{\frac{\Sigma\ d^2}{N}}$$

$$= \sqrt{\frac{120}{10}} \qquad\qquad = \sqrt{\frac{46}{10}}$$

$$= \sqrt{12} \qquad\qquad\qquad = \sqrt{4.6}$$

$$= \ 3.5\ \text{(app.)} \qquad\qquad = \ 2.2\ \text{(app.)}$$

Substituting in this formula the test scores from the two classes (Table 8–6), the values in Table 8–7 are obtained.

The following are the steps to obtain the standard deviation.

1. Find the deviation of each score from the mean ($d = X - M$). Give those scores below the mean a negative sign, and those above the mean a positive sign.
2. Square each deviation value (to get rid of the negative signs).
3. Find the sum of these squared deviations ($\Sigma\ d^2$).
4. Divide the $\Sigma\ d^2$ by N (the number of scores in each class, which in this example is 10).
5. Extract the square root of the above quotient (Step 4): this is the "standard deviation" (S.D.).

To aid in the understanding of this statistic, let us look at it in relationship to the normal or bell-shaped curve (Table 8–3). If we were to measure some human trait, such as height of a random sample of adult women, intelligence quotients of a random sample of 12-year-old boys, or the weight of babies at birth, we would most likely get this form of distribution. In this distribution, the number (frequencies) of scores should always be largest in the center, with the scores becoming fewer and fewer, like a bell, as we approach both extremes.

In the case of classroom testing with only 30 or 40 students, you must expect a lack of symmetry in your distribution. Unless the test is too easy or too hard, the results of your test should approximate a bell-shaped distribution, and the standard deviation becomes very useful.

Inspecting the normal curve of distribution, you will notice that the mean is erected from the baseline, and this vertical line divides the distribution into two equal parts. Vertical lines are also erected from the baseline to correspond to the different standard deviation units. These units are placed so that approximately 68 per cent of the total area of the curve is represented between −1 and +1 standard deviations from the mean. In the same manner, 95 per cent of the area lies between −2 and +2 standard deviations from the mean. Approximately 99 per cent of the test scores are between −3 and +3 standard deviation units from the mean. The percentage of cases with scores beyond ± 3 S.D. is negligible (see Figure 8–1).

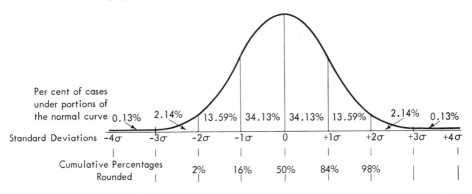

FIGURE 8–1. The Normal Curve.

Below these standard deviation unit values is a row of per cents which are in cumulative form. That is, they show the approximate percentage of people included to the left of each of the standard deviation units. For example, if a student scores one standard deviation above the mean, it can be concluded that his score ranks at the eighty-fourth percentile (the score representing the percentage of students who will fall below a given score) in the classroom.

MEASURES OF CORRELATION

In the statistical sense, correlation is the study of paired facts. For example, a teacher may wish to compare marks or scores obtained by her students in mathematics with those obtained in social studies. To be reliable, such comparisons should be based on marks or scores that are trustworthy. If the comparisons are based on unreliable scores they could be very misleading. Let us suppose that this comparison is based on reliable scores and the results shown in Table 8–8 are obtained for a class of ten eighth-grade students.

It is evident that Lori is first in both subjects, that Michael is second, Tom third, and so on down the class roster. This is shown by placing each student's rank after his score. It is evident that Table 8–8 illustrates a perfect positive relationship.

This relationship may also be represented graphically in the form of a scatter diagram or a bivariate distribution, such as is shown in Table 8–9.

It can be seen that when tabulated in this way (with the vertical class intervals set up with the highest at the top and the lowest at the bottom, and with the horizontal class intervals proceeding from the lowest at the left to the highest at the right), perfect positive correlation presents a straight line relationship extending from the upper right- to the lower left-hand

TABLE 8–8
Possible Results of an Objective Test Given to a Class of
Ten Eighth-Grade Students

| | Mathematics | | Social Studies | |
Students	Score	Rank	Score	Rank
Lori	34	1	76	1
Michael	33	2	72	2
Tom	30	3	66	3
Paul	28	4	63	4
Karen	25	5	60	5
Kathie	22	6	58	6
David	21	7	54	7
Gary	20	8	50	8
Jack	18	9	48	9
Kevin	16	10	44	10

TABLE 8–9
Illustrating Perfect Positive Relationship

Rank in Mathematics \ Rank in Social Studies	1	2	3	4	5	6	7	8	9	10
10										1
9									1	
8								1		
7							1			
6						1				
5					1					
4				1						
3			1							
2		1								
1	1									

corner of the table. Deviation from such correlation would result in a scattering of cases on both sides of this line, depending upon the amount of deviation.

Let us now suppose that the application of our tests in social studies and mathematics has given us a different result, such as illustrated in Table 8–10.

TABLE 8–10
Possible Results of an Objective Test Given to a Class of Ten Eighth-Grade Students

Students	Mathematics		Social Studies	
	Score	Rank	Score	Rank
Lori	34	1	44	10
Michael	33	2	48	9
Tom	30	3	50	8
Paul	28	4	54	7
Karen	25	5	58	6
Kathie	22	6	60	5
David	21	7	63	4
Gary	20	8	66	3
Jack	18	9	72	2
Kevin	16	10	76	1

It is evident that, in this example, the situation is exactly opposite from the one shown in the preceding illustration. Here Lori ranks first in mathematics but tenth in social studies, Michael ranks second in mathematics and ninth in social studies, and so on down the list. These distributions illustrate a perfect negative relationship.

When represented in the form of a scatter diagram, in the manner described for Table 8–9, we see that perfect negative correlation presents a straight line relationship extending from the upper left- to the lower right-hand corner of the table.

Tables such as 8–9 and 8–11 are useful in making rough estimates of the degree of relationship between two traits for which we have adequate measures. It is often desirable, however, to have a more precise statement of the amount of relationship than can be obtained by mere inspection. For this purpose a formula has been devised for computing the coefficient of correlation from such tables as 8–9 and 8–11. This formula enables us to state the amount of the relationship in exact numerical terms, ranging from $+1.00$ for a perfect positive relationship to a -1.00 for a perfect negative correlation. If there is no relation-

TABLE 8–11

Illustrating Perfect Negative Relationship

| | | Rank in Social Studies | | | | | | | | | |
		1	2	3	4	5	6	7	8	9	10
Rank in Mathematics	10	1									
	9		1								
	8			1							
	7				1						
	6					1					
	5						1				
	4							1			
	3								1		
	2									1	
	1										1

ship between the two sets of scores, i.e., one does not vary with the other in any way, the correlation coefficient is 0.00.

SUMMARY STATEMENT

The statistical methods and computations that have been presented are those most generally used by teachers whose primary concern is measuring and evaluating the progress of a classroom of students. The primary purpose of this chapter has been to give you an understanding of some of the basic statistical techniques, and to show how statistical analysis of a very elementary nature can be applied by any teacher to scores on a test in order to make the scores meaningful and therefore useful.

For those interested in a more extensive presentation of the techniques of statistical analysis, numerous statistic books are listed.

SUGGESTED READINGS

Bartz, A. E., *Elementary Statistical Methods for Educational Measurement.* Minneapolis, Minn.: Burgess Publishing Co., 1966. An excellent source for understanding basic statistical methods. Numerous illustrations are provided.

Blommers, P., and E. F. Lindquist, *Elementary Statistical Methods.* Boston: Houghton Mifflin Company, 1960. A general introductory treatment of statistical methods for students in education and psychology.

Cronbach, L. J., *Essentials of Psychological Testing* (2nd ed.). New York: Harper & Row, Publishers, 1960, Chap. 4. A discussion emphasizing theoretical aspects of statistical methods.

Edwards, A. L., *Statistical Analysis.* New York: Holt, Rinehart & Winston, Inc., 1958. A basic book on statistical methodology for the nonmathematically trained student.

Guilford, J. P., *Fundamental Statistics in Psychology and Education* (4th ed.). New York: McGraw-Hill Book Company, 1965. A standard reference work and a comprehensive text in the area of statistics.

Lyman, H. B., *Test Scores and What They Mean.* Englewood Cliffs, N.J.: Prentice-Hall, Inc., 1963. An excellent overview of the many ways in which a test score can be reported.

Manuel, H. T., *Elementary Statistics for Teachers.* New York: American Book Company, 1962. An introductory book on the statistics of educational measurement. Designed for students just beginning their study of statistics.

Thorndike, R. L., and E. Hagen, *Measurement and Evaluation in Psychology and Education*. New York: John Wiley & Sons, Inc., 1961, Chap. 5. This discussion points out to the student some basic types of questions that the statistician tries to answer, and presents the simplest methods used to answer them.

9

Assigning Grades:

The Paradoxes, the Inequities,

and the Plain Tomfooleries

The assigning of grades or marks during or at the end of a course is like a game. The students, who lack control over the system, must play the game according to rules that the teachers establish. If the teacher wants to give a number of low grades, all he has to do is give the same test to his college prep class and to his average class, and allot grades on the basis of a curve for the two classes. The "smaller team" certainly has the disadvantage.

A modification of this game is played in every classroom in every school throughout this country, and probably throughout the world, whenever grades have to be assigned. You have no doubt looked at this logic-defying question in other courses, but any discussion of appraisal procedures necessitates a kick or two at this proverbial beehive. This chapter will look at the purposes served by grades, whether grades actually represent how much a student knows, the sex differences in grades earned, the way teachers arrive at final grades and their students' views on the same subject, and a suggested way of arriving at final grades.

PURPOSES SERVED BY GRADES

Grading practices, although differing widely both within schools and among many schools throughout the country, attempt to provide data with which the student, his parents, teachers, and school administrators make important decisions affecting the student's current educational status and his future. In general, the following points represent the major purposes served by grades in the schools. The italics in the following have been added to point out the inherent shortcomings of these purposes.

1. Grades inform the student and his parents of how well he is progressing in the school (*according to the teacher*). This is usually the basis upon which parents and their children make decisions concerning future educational possibilities and vocational choices.

2. A grade presents a summary statement of the student's over-all achievement in a course (*I wish it did*). The most common practice is to report as one grade the combined grades students earn in several different activities, e.g., tests, homework assignments, book reports, discussions, *attitudes, and improvement*, throughout the course.

3. Grades present a convenient summary of a student's educational progress for college admissions officers and/or prospective employers. In both cases, a transcript of a student's total high school educational experience is of help (*unfortunately*) in making decisions concerning the student.

4. Grades also tend to be a motivating (*and also a defeating*) influence on too many high school students. The desire to make a high grade or to be on the honor roll influences the achievement of many students (*who therefore work for grades rather than "learning"*).

5. Grades present a convenient (*but misleading*) source of data for various types of curriculum studies.

DO FINAL GRADES INDICATE HOW MUCH
A STUDENT KNOWS OF THE SUBJECT?

Let us take another kick at the beehive to get both students' and teachers' ideas on this question. The rules of this game require the teacher to assign some symbol (usually a letter or number) to indicate the progress of each student toward the course objectives. This ritual usually takes place four times a year. There are some teachers who feel that the grades they assign a student represent how much the student knows of the subject.

> Properly designed tests should measure what a student has learned. I think my tests are properly designed. The final grade is based on test scores. (9th Grade, Algebra)

> Generally speaking, the final grade shows the results of the thinking process which is developed. (9th Grade, Fine Arts)

> A final grade in a subject is one indicator which furnishes a diagnosis of one student's capacities at one point in his life. (11th Grade, Science)

The majority of teachers, however, have mixed feelings as to the validity and reliability of their grading practices.

> To some extent, but not completely. To a large degree, the final grade represents the student's willingness to cooperate and try. (9th Grade, Remedial Reading)

> Ideally, they should but it may be that they crammed for the test and got the grade that way. (9th Grade, Science)

> Not entirely. The grade always has some subjective judgment built in. They're probably not too valid. (11th Grade, U.S. History)

> No, they represent what he knows that the teacher wanted him to know. He may learn many other things in the class that are not graded. (9th Grade, Math)

Students are not split on their attitudes as sharply as the teachers. Most of them have very strong feelings concerning how the grade is arrived at and the things that can affect the grade they receive.

> He just bunches everything together and averages it out. So, you don't know what's what. You just know that it's your grade for the quarter. (8th Grade, English)

> I don't think so because when we have an objective test, I study real hard and get good grades, but I'm a lousy

typist. My grade is higher than it should be. I forget it all as soon as the test is over. (10th Grade, Typing I)

Actually it would depend a great deal on your teacher. If for some reason there was a personality conflict or a problem between a student and teacher your grade will depend a lot on feelings your teacher thinks you have toward learning. (12th Grade, American Government)

No. I go a whole grade down on the final exam. It makes me all upset. (10th Grade, Geometry)

No. We don't get a chance to tell all we know. (7th Grade, Core)

Some kids get good grades because they memorize and study just for grades. Some learn more because they try and make sense out of the material. (12th Grade, Home-making)

I don't think it completely tells. You can be taught a lot and a teacher can't test on everything, only a sampling. You may study one thing, maybe the thing the teacher will test you on or maybe not. You may get sick. I don't feel grades tell the whole story. (11th Grade, Science)

Much of the confusion about grades can be traced to the fact that these grades are used by teachers for many different reasons, and no one definition is able to cover all the factors involved. Teachers do not agree on a standard meaning and freely admit that they use different criteria in appraising student achievement. Among the more commonly used criteria are test scores, teacher-student relationship, deportment, sex, promptness, obedience, effort, and attitude.

The one criterion common to all grades is the actual achievement of students in the subject matter for which they are being graded. The other criteria are usually subjective appraisals. The degree to which these subjective appraisals help determine the grade a student receives is not completely known.

What can be done to make grading a more valid and reliable indicator of student performance? You are caught in the paradox of periodically having to assign grades to students in your class throughout the school year. It is the rule of the game. The following sections of this chapter will hopefully provide some insights for making the "grading game" more meaningful for you and the students in your classes.

SEX DIFFERENCES IN GRADING

Throughout the years, the literature has provided lively discussions relative to the influence of a student's sex on school grades. Some of it has been conjecture and some of it actual findings of measurable relationships. C. C. Ross, for example, stated in his book[1] :

> It seems too bad that the marks received by certain individuals are conditioned more by the contours of the face than by the contents of the head.

The justification for this statement is quite evident in the literature. Garner,[2] for example, attempted to compare the grades that had been assigned by men and women teachers. His data were obtained by investigating 5,152 marks assigned to boys and 5,132 marks assigned to girls. He made no attempt to differentiate the school subjects, and concluded that both the men and women teachers give high marks to girls rather than to boys.

Another article investigated the membership of the National Honor Society at Lindsborg, Kansas, High School for the years 1932–1941.[3] In this study, the investigator found that, even though boys outnumbered girls in class attendance for the ten-year period, girls outnumbered boys in the Honor Society by 2.75 to 1. Swenson did not find substantial differences in the intelligence of the boys and girls, and decided that membership was gained by inequalities in teachers' marks. He concluded teachers were prejudiced against boys. The comments of a twelfth-grade student would tend to confirm this conclusion.

> Women teachers are always after boys to shut up and men teachers think they're your father. I don't think girls get all that kind of stuff.

Additional insight is gained in this area by Edmiston's study.[4]

[1] C. C. Ross, *Measurement in Today's Schools*, 2nd ed. (Englewood Cliffs, N.J.: Prentice-Hall, Inc., 1947), p. 405.

[2] C. E. Garner, "Survey of Teachers' Marks," *School and Community*, 21 (1935), 116–117.

[3] C. Swenson, "Packing the Honor Society," *Clearing House*, 16 (1942) 521–524.

[4] R. W. Edmiston, "Do Teachers Show Partiality Toward Boys or Girls?" *Peabody Journal of Education*, 20 (1943), 234–238.

In the school which he studied, the average grade for girls was 84.4, while for boys it was 80.0. He further pointed out that women teachers gave the girls grades that averaged 5.4 points above those given to boys, while men teachers were less partial to the girls, giving them an average of only 3.4 points more than was given to boys.

Lobaugh[5] investigated the relationship of standardized achievement test scores and grades assigned by teachers. He found that girls had a grade point average of 2.19, while the boys had a grade point average of only 1.97. When he compared the scores made on the Myer-Ruch High School Progress Test, the boys' median score was 46, while the median score for girls was 36. Lobaugh accounted for the differences between achievement and marks on the basis that girls were more meticulous, more punctual, and neater about their work. He also recognized greater maturity among the girls and a tendency for the boys to compensate for their immaturity.

Carter[6] asked himself the question, "With intelligence held constant, what is the relationship between the sex of the student and the sex of the teacher in the assignment of marks in beginning algebra?" In investigating this problem, significant differences were observed. Girls made significantly higher marks than did boys. Women teachers tended to give higher marks than did the men teachers. Specifically, when marks were assigned, boys were given lower marks than were the girls, regardless of whether the teacher was a man or a woman; but marks assigned by men teachers were generally lower than marks assigned by women teachers. These data indicate a definite necessity for the refining of grades if these are to reflect true achievement.

Let us leave the journals and ask some teachers and students who are presently in school what they think about the issue. The following is an illustration of the views of a twelfth-grade English teacher and three students in one of her classes.

> *Teacher*:   Girls tend to act out less than boys even when they're not particularly good students and therefore the boys might find it harder to please on a test or a homework assignment. Now that I think about it I guess I'm

[5]D. Lobaugh, "Girls, Grades, and IQ's," *Nation Schools*, 30 (1942), 42.
[6]R. S. Carter, "How Invalid are Marks Assigned by Teachers?" *Journal of Educational Psychology*, 43 (1952), 218–228.

harder on boys for just that reason; particularly if they've given me trouble in class.

Student: Girls always butter the teacher up and give out with flattery and make it sound like they care, but it usually goes over pretty bad with a boy, if it's a woman teacher, she usually thinks you're a phony. It doesn't work at all for a boy with a man teacher. (Boy)

Student: Boys usually have a harder time writing than girls. I think boys are more able in thinking out loud than putting things on paper. In English with a young woman teacher who's not used to loud mouth boys, a girl who is willing to talk in discussions can do better. (Girl)

Student: I think it's harder for a boy to get onto what a woman teacher wants from her students. Most men teachers usually are pretty tough on boys—they expect a lot out of them. (Girl)

What are some of the other factors teachers feel contribute to this disparity between grades assigned to girls and to boys?

Girls are more mature at this grade level (seventh and eighth). More prestige in grades for a girl at this age. Girls are more conforming. (7th Grade, Core)

Girls find it easier to conform and tend to do more of the busy-work than boys. (9th Grade, Math)

Girls are usually more mature and have more mature study habits—because of this they may get higher grades. (9th Grade, General Science)

Girls are more cooperative and tend to please teachers, which might influence grades. (9th Grade, Algebra)

They are more apt to follow instructions and do their homework. (10th Grade, World History)

Girls are more able to adapt to the controls and restrictions that the school imposes. (Remedial Reading)

An eleventh-grade English teacher sums up this area quite nicely. "I think the high school is oriented to the female mind and the colleges to the male mind. The approach (in the high school) is more appealing to the girl. In this adolescent period, girls are more open in getting out their problems, and the problems don't interfere with school work."

METHODS OF ASSIGNING GRADES

Although there is some evidence to support it, this chapter's intent is not to condemn all grading practices and demand their immediate revision, but to indicate that marking procedures are necessarily only as good or as bad as the teacher who is trying to apply them. The teacher, who by the rules of the game must evaluate many students periodically, should be aware of the difficulties central to this very important area of teacher-student relations. He should look upon this dilemma as a challenge of good teaching, i.e., to strive for objective, accurate evaluations of students in learning situations.

Strange as it may sound, students tend to accept the rules of the game while it is being played, even though they may be chopped down during it. You are the teacher and can set the rules any way you want. Once the grades are entered into the grade book, however, they become quite sensitive and want a "fair shake" when you average all of the points for the final grade. Many will question you on your procedures or argue the case for a higher grade if they feel they were unjustly treated. It is up to you to explain, demonstrate, or even refigure their points to show them how you arrived at their grade. Under these circumstances a teacher should have a well thought out procedure for arriving at final grades.

Muessig endorses this point by saying that a school grade has many meanings.[7] "Must grades and report cards remain enveloped by ancient ambiguity, medieval mysticism, or contemporary conjuring? Can their hidden meanings be unlocked for all to see and understand, or must they be the secret of the 'teacher magician'?" He goes on to say that each teacher should work out his unique philosophy of grading, put it down on paper, study it carefully, revise it, and come up with a thorough policy with which he is willing to live.

A number of people have been advocating the elimination of number or letter grades in recent years. The Pass-Fail, or Pass-No Pass, system is being used increasingly in the secondary

---

[7]R. H. Muessig, "The Mystery of Grading and Reporting," *Education*, 83 (1962), 92.

schools. This system does not offer a panacea. The teacher is still required to make a judgment as to what constitutes a Pass or Fail grade.

Since few people are willing to accept a truly gradeless system in the schools, they should strive to find the most equitable method for all concerned. Tees points out that, regardless of the type of grading systems used, the problem remains making the methods of evaluation accurately reflect the student's performance.[8]

Grading by Inspection   This is a method of assigning grades which is widely used by classroom teachers, but not readily admitted. In this process, the teacher examines the distribution of total scores earned by the class in hopes of finding "gaps" or "cutoff points." When these numerical areas in which there are no student scores are found, the teacher draws a line to indicate that the scores above have earned such and such a grade. An example might be as shown in the table.

In this method, the distribution determines the percentage of marks to be assigned. The major criticism addressed to this

Grading by Inspection

Student	Score	Grade
Lori	158	
Mike	153	A
Karen	150	
Jack	144	
David	143	
Paul	142	
Tom	142	B
Cathy	140	
Kevin	139	
Gary	128	
Kindra	127	
Barbara	123	
Judy	123	C
Bill	122	
Bob	120	
George	119	
Rose	111	
Jack	109	D

[8]A. T. Tees, "In Defense of Grades," *School and Community*, 55 (1968), 12.

method is that the assignment of grades is completely arbitrary. It does not take into consideration such things as the unreliability of these gaps in the distribution, the variance of the total scores, or similar data from previous class performances in order to judge the status and progress of students in the current class. In other words, if this method is to be used, some reference point is needed to gauge the performance of the class group.

Grading on a Curve   This is probably the most often used and least understood method. In its use, grades are assigned according to the relative standing of students in your classroom. The characteristics of the normal, or bell-shaped, curve are used in determining the number of each grade assigned. The large group of students who receive scores in the middle of the distribution will receive the average grade, while relatively few at the extremes will earn the high and low marks. One common procedure for determining the cutting scores for the various grade distributions is by the standard deviation distance based on the characteristics of the theoretical normal curve as shown in the figure. In other words, students who earn a C extend from one-half a standard deviation on both sides of the mean, and include approximately 38 per cent of the total group. The B and D groups extend one standard deviation beyond these limits, and each includes another 24 per cent of the total group. The two extreme groups, A and F, are located between ± 1.5 S.D. and ± 2.5 S.D., and include approximately 7 per cent more of the class.

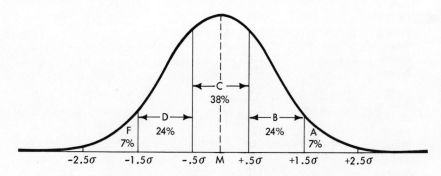

Distribution of Marks Based on Standard Deviation.

Even though it sounds objective and impartial, this method assumes that the distribution of points in a classroom follows roughly the characteristics of the theoretical normal curve. In reality, the distribution of points made by a class of 35 rarely, if ever, approaches this ideal, in that a class is only a sample from a larger group, e.g., all eleventh-grade students in a district, in which the scores would be distributed normally. In working with our class, we assume that the mean and standard deviation are the same for our class as for the larger group. This assumption cannot be made.

Furthermore, if your classes are homogeneously grouped, this method of assigning grades would be improper. The distribution of points for a college prep class would undoubtedly look something like the curve shown in the second figure. How could you

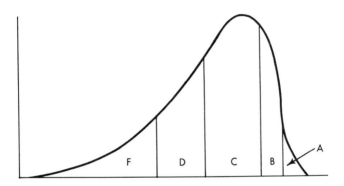

Distribution of Marks Based on a Skewed Curve.

justify to a student or his parents the assigned grade of C in this type of a distribution?

To employ group curves as the standard for an individual's achievement is to guess the achievement of the individual. Strom makes the statement, "It is fair to say that the concept of individual differences has been employed least in the area where it is most needed; namely the assessment of achievement."[9] When students must view grades as an index of their work-product rank in relation to their fellow students rather than as rough indices to denote whether they are progressing in their course, it is natural that pursuit of grades will come to occupy a prime position, while learning itself is secondary. As a result, scholarship is dealt a severe blow and overly strong attitudes of rivalry and competition are set up.

[9]R. D. Strom, "Academic Achievement and Mental Health," *Journal of Secondary Education*, 39 (1964), 349.

Many teachers who use the "grading on a curve" method use what they call a "modified curve." This usually means introducing subjective judgments in their determination of grades. A ninth-grade teacher explains her method this way.

> I average homework grades, quizzes, and tests. I consider class participation, and conduct. I ask myself if this grade really represents what this student seems to know. I adjust it as necessary.

Often teachers base the marks they give their students on factors other than student achievement of the objectives of instruction. One of the major requirements of a good grading system is that the grades indicate as accurately as possible the degree to which the student has achieved the instructional objectives in a particular course. If improving the student's attitude toward American History is one of the objectives of the course, and the teacher has planned specific methods to attain this objective, then it should be considered in assigning grades. Unfortunately, this is not always the case. All too often, subjective judgments involving unnecessary talking in the classroom, attitude toward the teacher, attentiveness, or personal appearance are used by the teacher in assigning grades. Subjective judgments that have no bearing on the objectives of instruction must be limited, as they can easily distort the intended meaning of the grade.

A Suggested Procedure for Computing a Final Grade   To arrive at a final grade for a student, the teacher must usually bring together and average the grades or points the student has earned in a number of class activities. By using the specific objectives for the particular class, the teacher has identified those classroom activities that will be used in determining the students' grades. The teacher, however, must also determine the relative importance of each assignment with regard to his specific instructional objectives. After this relative importance is determined, a "numerical weight" is assigned to each of the activities to be considered, so that the importance, or lack of importance, is transferred to the final grade. For example, suppose Lori earned the grades shown in the table throughout a semester of World History.

Hypothetical Grades Earned in One Semester of World History

Activity	Grade and Grade Points		Weight Factor	Score Points
First exam	C	(2)	2	4
Second exam	A	(4)	2	8
Term paper	B	(3)	3	9
Oral report	B	(3)	1	3
Book report	C	(2)	1	2
Final exam	A	(4)	4	16
Class recitation	B	(3)	1/2	1 1/2
Total			13 1/2	43 1/2

In this example, each of the student's letter grades are converted into points. The teacher's subjective judgment as to the quality of Lori's recitation in the class was given a letter grade and transformed into point values. The most common method for assigning points is to convert an A to four points, a B to three points, a C to two points, a D to one point, and an F to zero points. The column labeled *Weight Factor* refers to the weight value of each grade. In other words, the teacher determines the relative importance of each activity and assigns a weight to it. In the example, the final exam is weighted twice as heavily as each of the two earlier classroom exams. The term paper is weighted three times as much as the book report and the oral report, and six times as much as class recitation.

After making these entries, the teacher, by using the "total" figures, determines the "average score points" earned by the student. For example, Lori earned a total of 43½ score points with a total weight factor of 13½. The average score points are a quotient resulting from the division of 43½ score points by 13½, or 3.22.

The range of the average score points in this grading procedure is generally as follows for grades A through F:

A: 3.5–4.0   points
B: 2.5–3.49   points
C: 1.5–2.49   points
D: 0.5–1.49   points
F: 0.0–0.49   points

This suggested method for computing final grades can be done quickly and may include any class activity you feel important enough to be reflected in the final grade. It satisfies the criteria of objectivity and accuracy which are necessary to the evaluation of students in a learning situation.

SUMMARY STATEMENT

School grades are partly fancy and partly fact. Unfortunately, it appears that some student grades are more fancy than fact. The teacher must constantly battle to be alert to the pitfalls and difficulties which are inherent in the grading process. It is felt that awareness of these problems should make for better grading practices. Each teacher should strive for accurate and objective evaluations of pupil work and progress.

SUGGESTED READINGS

Ahmann, J. S., and M. D. Glock, *Evaluating Pupil Growth* (3rd ed.). Boston: Allyn & Bacon, Inc., 1967, Chap. 16. A thorough discussion covering many areas, e.g., reporting to parents, methods of assigning grades, and student-teacher conferences, concerning the problem of determining and reporting student growth.

Brown, B. F., *The Non-Graded High School.* Englewood Cliffs, N.J.: Prentice-Hall, Inc., 1963. The non-graded high school at Melbourne, Florida, is described. One of the topics discussed is the marking and reporting of grades in the non-graded school.

Ebel, R. L., *Measuring Educational Achievement.* Englewood Cliffs, N.J.: Prentice-Hall, Inc., 1965, Chap. 13. The principal ideas developed in this chapter are summarized in 27 statements.

Jarret, C. D., "Marking and Reporting Practices in the American Secondary School," *Peabody Journal of Education,* 41 (1963), 36–48. The author contends that marking systems are often antidemocratic. The argument for final marks which show individual growth and against competitive marks is presented.

Lindvall, C. M., *Testing and Evaluation: An Introduction.* New York: Harcourt, Brace & World, Inc., 1961, App. Discusses the shortcomings of the current grading practices. Makes a plea for some standard that would indicate what each of the grades means throughout a school or a school system.

Remmers, H. H., N. L. Gage, and J. F. Rummel, *A Practical Introduction to Measurement and Evaluation.* New York: Harper & Row, Publishers, 1965, Chap. 9. A presentation covering the nature of school marks, the bases of marking systems, methods of assigning marks, combining marks for final grades, and types of reporting practices.

Stodola, Q., and K. Stordahl, *Basic Educational Tests and Measurement*. Chicago: Science Research Associates, Inc., 1967, pp. 46–52. A discussion of ways tests can be used to evaluate student achievement and the assignment of grades.

10

Published Tests:

An Evil or a Blessing?

Today's teachers are expected to find their way through a maze of intelligence quotients, achievement percentiles, and enough other specialized test language to make their heads spin. As a result, many teachers misunderstand, misinterpret, and abuse published, or standardized, test results. This leads to educational mishaps that may have a disastrous effect on a student.

> The school uses the test for placement without giving you any choice sometimes. You may get a score just by chance. I had to take Algebra I because I got a 96 on my eighth grade Iowa test. I flunked out because I was too slow and always behind the class. I shouldn't have been forced to take the class. (Senior)

If this is the case, just what purpose does this "standardized testing" serve over and above the purposes served by the teachers' own tests, and what are the implications for the students and the schools? To attempt an answer to this question, it would be well to begin by trying to understand what a standardized test is and how it differs from the teacher-made test.

1. The standardized test is a much more carefully designed and devised instrument, both in the selection of content and with respect to the specific questions that make it up. There has grown up in the past 50 years a considerable body of knowledge about how to write better tests, and the standardized test is prepared by persons who have made a special study of this technology of examination building.

2. The standardized test is given according to uniform procedures so that all students who take it are confronted with essentially the same task, and their performance is rated according to some well-defined set of rules.

3. The standardized test, in the course of its development, is administered to large and supposedly representative groups of pupils across the nation whose scores are compiled and summarized so that the performance of any particular student can be compared with scores of other students of his own age or grade or particular type of educational experience. It is the availability of these statistics, or *norms*, that make the standardized test a uniquely useful tool.

There are many different standardized tests which serve a variety of purposes and seek to measure a wide variety of abilities or scholastic attainments. For our purposes, two general kinds of standardized tests which represent the types most frequently used in the junior and senior high schools will be discussed. The first of these is the so-called intelligence test, and the second is the achievement test which measures how well the student has mastered various skills or bodies of information taught by the majority of schools throughout the country.

INTELLIGENCE TESTS

"Intelligence test" has become a household phrase; there are few college students who have not themselves taken this type of test. In a general way, therefore, you are all familiar with one or more intelligence tests. A more clear-cut understanding of the nature of these tests and the reasons for their use is vital for teachers.

In some respects, "intelligence test" is a misnomer, or at least a poor label for this type of test. Psychologists are far from in agreement as to just what intelligence is, or indeed if there is any single characteristic of humans that may properly be labeled intelligence. In addition, the tests called "intelligence" do not always measure the same things and, consequently, the score from one does not always agree with a score from another. The term "intelligence," moreover, carries for most people a suggestion of a more or less fixed, unvarying, probably hereditary characteristic, but no intelligence test maker, to my knowledge, believes that whatever his test measures has any of these properties. It is better to think of intelligence tests as measures of scholastic aptitude, academic progress, or academic potential.

Just what is an intelligence test like? What kinds of questions does a typical test include? First, a typical question from a so-called intelligence test used in the primary grades involves a row of pictures. The student is directed to mark the one of four which does not belong with the others. The test is made up of a series of such panels.

What does a child have to do in working his way through a test of this kind? He must, first of all, be able to attend to the task; he must have a measure of visual-perceptual ability sufficient to permit him to identify similarities and dissimilarities among several drawings; he must, in some questions, be able to bring to bear a certain amount of information as to the nature and use of pictured objects; he must be able to abstract certain common properties from several pictured objects and to form generalizations; he must be able to sustain his attention for a period of 20 to 30 minutes required for the test; he must follow directions. In short, he must use a wide variety of abilities that most educators would agree are fundamentally intellectual in character and of importance for school work. It should be pointed out that the tasks which the student is called upon to perform are not tasks that he has specifically been taught in the average school. Also of importance is the fact that at this age level these types of tests make no demand on reading ability, so that even a child at the elementary school level with a language handicap is penalized little, if any, in his performance.

As a student reaches the upper grades and high school, however, the so-called intelligence tests become verbal tests. They involve reading and begin to presuppose mastery of certain language and numerical skills that have, indeed, been taught in school. Such tests include questions that seek to measure the same aspects of mental functioning, together with some others, as the primary test. Their questions take the form of vocabulary questions, problem-solving questions, arithmetical reasoning and numerical skills questions, and analogies questions which attempt to get at the student's ability to see relationships and to apply these relationships to new contexts and form generalizations.

In order to illustrate the areas typically covered in a group intelligence test, sample items from the widely used Lorge-Thorndike Intelligence Test are reproduced below.[1]

This test contains a verbal battery and a nonverbal battery. The verbal section has five subtests measuring Word Knowledge, Sentence Completion, Verbal Classification, Verbal Analogies, and Arithmetic Reasoning. The nonverbal section has three subtests which measure Figure Analogies, Figure Classification, and Number Series. Illustrations of each of these subtests are presented below.

Verbal Battery

Test 1:   Word Knowledge

For each exercise in this test you are to read the word in dark type at the beginning of that exercise. Then, from the five words that follow you are to choose the word that has the same meaning or most nearly the same meaning as the word in dark type. Look at sample exercise O.

O. **LOUD**   A. quick   B. noisy   C. hard   D. heavy
           E. weak

The words are arranged in ascending order of difficulty, i.e., easy words first and most difficult at the end of the subtest. They cover a variety of areas of human experience and knowledge. A high score on this test would indicate that the student is widely read. However, there might be students with knowledge of words not represented on this test.

Test 2:   Sentence Completion

In each exercise in this test, a word has been left out of a sentence. Read the sentence carefully; then, from the five words that follow, choose the one word that will make the best, the truest, and the most sensible complete sentence. Look at sample exercise O.

O.   Hot weather comes in the _____.

     A. fall   B. night   C. summer   D. winter   E. snow

[1]Reproduced from *Lorge-Thorndike Intelligence Tests* (Boston: Houghton Mifflin Company, © 1964), by permission of the publisher.

In this test, besides knowing the right word, the student must see relationships. The sentences and the words presented become increasingly more difficult in the course of the test. A high score on this test would indicate the student's ability to see relationships and his general reading background.

Test 3: Arithmetic Reasoning

In this test you are to work some arithmetic problems. After each problem are four possible answers and a fifth choice, "none of these," meaning that the answer is not given. Work each problem and compare your answer with the four possible answers. If the correct answer is given, fill in the space on the answer sheet that has the same letter as the right answer. If the correct answer is not given, fill in the space on the answer sheet that has the same letter as "none of these." Look at the illustration.

OOO.   At an auction, a store owner bought a number of rugs for $700. He sold the rugs one by one, receiving $1300. He made an average of $50 per rug. How many rugs did he originally buy?

A. 50   B. 21   C. 28   D. 38   E. none of these

The wording of the problems is simple and clear and the vocabulary should not stand in the way of solving the problems correctly.

Test 4:   Verbal Classification

For each exercise in this test, a series of words is given in dark type. You are to figure out how the words in dark type are alike, then you are to choose the one word among the five on the line below that belongs with the words in dark type. Look at sample exercise OO.

OO.   **GO   RUN   WALK   MOVE**

A. think   B. dream   C. march   D. sing   E. seem

As can be seen by the directions, this is a test of a student's ability to see relationships as well as a test of vocabulary.

Test 5:   Word Analogies

For each exercise in this test, a pair of words is given that are related to each other in some way. Look at the first two words and figure out how they are related to each other. Then, from the five words on the line below, choose the word that is related to the third in the same way. Look at sample exercise OO.

OO.   chair —→ sit : bed —→

  A. lie   B. bedroom   C. night   D. crib   E. tired

This is a test of relationships, vocabulary, and general knowledge. The vocabulary becomes more difficult as the test progresses.

Nonverbal Battery

While the instructions for each of the three subtests in the nonverbal section are written in the test booklets, they are also read by the test administrator to decrease, to a certain extent, the influence of students' verbal facility on the scores the students earn on these tests.

Test 1:   Figure Classification

For each exercise in this test, a series of drawings is given which are alike in a certain way. You are to figure out in what way the drawings are alike. Then you are to find the drawing at the right that goes with the first group. Look at sample exercise O. The first three drawings in the row are alike in a certain way. Find the drawing at the right that goes with the first three.

O.
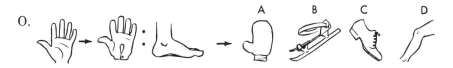

Test 2:   Number Series

For each exercise in this test a series of numbers or letters is given in a certain order. You are to figure out the order (or way) in which the series of numbers is arranged, then find the number or letter at the right that should come next. Look at sample exercise OO.

OO.   5   5   4   4   3   A. 1   B. 2   C. 3   D. 4   E. 5

Test 3:   Figure Analogies

In each exercise in this test, the first two drawings go

together in a certain way. You are to figure out how the first two go together, then find the drawing at the right that goes with the third drawing in the same way that the second goes with the first. Look at sample exercise O.

O.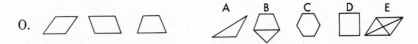

Each of these subtests involves identifying the given relationships and selecting the appropriate response to maintain the presented relationship.

The Lorge-Thorndike Intelligence Test is a series of tests of abstract intelligence. Abstract intelligence is defined by the authors of the test as the ability to work with ideas and the relationships among ideas. The tests are based on the premise that since most abstract ideas with which the student deals are expressed in verbal symbols, verbal symbols are the appropriate medium for the testing of abstract intelligence. Nevertheless, the authors attempt to take into account the fact that for some, e.g., the poor reader or the poorly educated, printed words may constitute an inadequate basis for appraising individual abilities. Consequently, a parallel set of nonverbal tests is provided to accompany the verbal series.

Why is the classroom teacher, or the principal, or the school system generally interested in measuring the intelligence or scholastic aptitude of students? The primary reason is that the teacher can do a far better job of suiting his instruction to the particular level of student ability when he has dependable information as to what that level is. He can set more realistic goals for the student and can judge more accurately the probable rate at which it is reasonable to expect that particular student to learn. If a student is experiencing learning difficulties, it is very helpful for a teacher to have some idea as to whether the problem is one of general level of mental ability, some particular learning difficulty in a given subject, or some other type of problem.

I use the test scores when I suspect a student is not capable of handling the work. I come in and check his test scores. However, it might be a personality conflict. Maybe he doesn't like me and isn't going to perform for me, and many students are immature enough to take this attitude. If I suspect that a student can't handle the work and is over-achieving, or if I suspect that a student can handle the work and is under-achieving, I come and check the scores and see if he does have the ability to handle the work. (11th Grade, English)

This information about the students becomes of importance to supervisors and administrators in planning the curriculum, in assessing the need for various types of courses and learning experiences, and in evaluating the effectiveness of the instructional programs. The school administration cannot make a realistic approach to their responsibilities without a continuing picture of the quality of the student population with which they must deal.

Many school districts go a little further in their uses of intelligence test scores, some of which are not supported by many adults and high school students. A recent article reported the results of a survey regarding the use of test information.[2] Brim surveyed 1,500 adults and 10,000 high school students. One of the questions asked was: "Given tests as they now are, do you think it is fair to use intelligence tests to help make the following decisions?"

1. To decide who can go to certain colleges?
   41 per cent of adults opposed—54 per cent of students opposed
2. To put students in special classes in schools?
   25 per cent of adults opposed—50 per cent of students opposed
3. To decide who should be hired for a job?
   37 per cent of adults opposed—53 per cent of students opposed
4. To decide who should be promoted?
   50 per cent of adults opposed—67 per cent of students opposed.

All too often, the test score is used without inquiring into the students' motivation, anxiety, and the physical facilities used at the administration of the test. These factors affect the scores to a considerable degree. The following are student comments which illustrate this point.

[2]L. F. Carter, "Psychological Testing and Public Responsibility," *Science*, 146, No. 3642, (1964), 1687–1695.

I am tense when taking these tests and do not do well. (Senior)

The questions kind of stun you for a minute. Should have been in the classroom rather than the auditorium. Some kids mess around all the time and you can't keep your mind on it. (Junior)

Weren't very good conditions. All crowded together and distracting. (Freshman)

Worried. I could just see people looking at my scores and saying how dumb I am. I guess I just don't like the proof laying around. (Senior)

I don't think the test really showed anything because I wasn't trying to prove anything. (Senior)

Results of the so-called intelligence tests are usually expressed in the form of the IQ (Intelligence Quotient). The IQ is a test score, and like any test score it is neither infallible nor inflexible. It is not an index of some hereditary trait, nor does it pretend to measure such important features as creativity, artistic talent, initiative, or anything other than scholastic academic aptitude.

The IQ of a student usually changes as he progresses through school, which is why many school systems administer these tests at regular intervals. The surprising thing is that the changes from one testing to another are not greater than they are; drastic shifts that would cause radical reevaluation of the student's academic talent are the exception and not the rule.

It is also true that IQ's derived from different tests vary to an extent that can mislead and confuse even the most alert teacher. These tests differ in the aspects of the mental ability they measure, in the reliability with which these aspects are measured, and in the nature of the norming sample used to derive the IQ. It is best to do away with the idea of *the* IQ; there is *an* IQ from a particular test administered at a given time under specific circumstances.

Intelligence test scores are essential to educational planning because they are, in some measure, an indication of how well a student will succeed in school. They also give school personnel a quick tool with which they can discriminate between the ablest and the least able student in the school. Teachers, however, should be cautious about using a single test score; they should make use of it as an estimate rather than a literally exact measure of intelligence. Teachers should study the complete record of the student and be slow in drawing any but tentative conclusions until sufficient data are available upon which a decision can be reached. A single IQ is a potentially dangerous piece of information unless its values and limitations are fully understood.

In reporting intelligence, the grade level of the student should be considered in what is reported and the terms in which it is reported. Intelligence is less reliably measured at the early ages; moreover, the primary student may not have had the advantage of more than one intelligence measure, while students in the later grades have had the confirmation of several such tests. In addition to this lower certainty of the true mental ability of the younger student, there is less necessity for a parent to have any definite measure of a young child's intelligence. When educational choices, such as high school courses and college plans, and vocational considerations come into the picture, they reflect a situation as of a given time which is subject to change. Also, parents, in some cases, lack a basis for interpreting an Intelligence Quotient; some cannot be restrained from considering them as more exact and final than they really are, and many are unable to accept certain relatively low measures objectively. Moreover, not all schools are able to provide the individual counseling that is needed for such reporting.

In general, it is best to report in terms of *levels* rather than of definite numerical scores, particularly in the case of intelligence test results. One must always take into account the fact that each test score estimàtes with some specified degree of accuracy the true score. No test is perfectly reliable, so that the resulting score is an approximation. On another day with another test, or even a different form of the same test, the scores would probably not be exactly the same. Interpretation of individual scores should always take into account this error of measurement.

ACHIEVEMENT TESTS

The second type of standardized test we will consider is the achievement test. In this category are tests of reading, arithmetic, spelling, world history, biology—tests that measure the extent to which students have attained proficiency in any of the great variety of subjects and courses offered in the schools. Throughout the grades, there is usually systematic testing that measures the student's progress and growth in fundamental subjects. These tests, by virtue of their norms, enable the teacher to judge at what achievement level a student is reading, at what grade level his language ability is, or how he compares with representative students across the country in his attainment of mastery in such subjects as American history or physics. These standardized tests in no sense take the place of the teacher's own appraisal and evaluation of the work of his students. They supplement the teacher's observation by providing a measure that is less affected by the many elements which consciously or unconsciously creep into a teacher's own appraisal. In other words, they give the teacher an independent yardstick with which to evaluate the progress each of his students is making.

Because these tests are developed in the form of a series covering a wide range of grades, they offer possibilities for continuous measurement of growth and development that are simply not possible through the typical teacher-made examination. Again, because of the normative information, these tests permit more accurate comparisons of a student's performance in the various subjects than is possible with teacher-made tests, and thus provide, for guidance purposes, more dependable information on the student's strengths and weaknesses.

The principal objective of the standardized achievement tests is to measure an individual's or group of individuals' attainment of commonly accepted educational objectives. More specifically, the functions that these tests most commonly serve in the secondary school include the following:

1. They provide a measure of relative standing in particular skills or subject-matter areas for a student, a class, or a school.
2. They provide dependable measures of student progress toward desirable educational goals.
3. These tests provide measures revealing a student's relative strengths or weaknesses in subject areas which are of significance for guidance purposes.
4. They provide "diagnostic-type" information which permits a sharper definition of learning difficulties and enables instruction to be brought to bear more forcefully on points where it is most needed.
5. These tests are one source of data for evaluating the adequacy of the school's instructional program.

They are, in a word, fact-finding devices. Like any other type of test, the standardized achievement tests are a means to an end and not an end in themselves. They provide the teacher, the supervisor, and the administrator with only partial information which must be supplemented by other data, such as the student's mental ability, interests, and previous grades. Used effectively, these tests provide a rich source for the kind of data on which sound evaluation must depend.

Standardized achievement tests may be classified into two general types. First is the subject-matter test, which provides a comprehensive evaluation of a student's attainment in a single subject, e.g., chemistry, second-year algebra, or general science. These tests provide the teacher with an over-all picture of a student's standing in relationship to other members of his class. This general type of test should not be confused with a "diagnostic-type" test which is commonly used at the elementary school level. The coverage of the subject matter is too broad to identify specific strengths and weaknesses of a student. The subject-matter tests will, however, give some indication of a student's *general* strengths and weaknesses in the subject area.

The other type is the survey battery. As the name implies, the survey battery is designed to measure the attainment of a student or a group of students in a number of subject-matter areas represented in the school curriculum. This battery contains a number of subject-matter tests which can be administered separately or together. For example, a survey battery designed for the secondary school may include tests for English, reading, science, social studies, arts and humanities, and writing. Most of the survey batteries provide a profile on which a student's score is plotted graphically, so that a teacher is able to determine the student's relative strengths and weaknesses in each area.

With the diversity of junior and senior high school courses, the differing content and emphases in courses with the same name, and the differing class schedules throughout the country, the authors of achievement tests have had to resolve interschool differences in one of two ways. The first and most widely used method is to base the test on only such content and skills as are represented in the most widely used textbooks for each subject area to be measured. The other practice is to construct a test that measures the student's ability to apply knowledge and skills that he has learned in a given instructional sequence to realistic situations.

Few of the current survey batteries can be categorized as representing one type or the other; most of them employ both practices in their construction. It is difficult to conceive a test measuring just application without some attention being paid to specific skills and knowledge upon which application skills or interpretative ability are based.

What kind of questions should a typical survey achievement

battery contain? What are the subject areas that are included? The following test questions are from the Stanford Achievement Test, High School Battery, which was recently published by Harcourt, Brace & World.[3]

Numerical Competence   This test is designed to measure general mathematical competence, emphasizing arithmetical and numerical competence. An example of a test item in this area follows.

(Use the table below to answer questions 35–37)

Shooting Record of the Members of a Basketball Team

Player	Shots Attempted	Shots Made
Jones	27	11
Smith	5	0
Allen	18	8
Lyons	11	5
Olson	14	2

35. The five players as a team made approximately what per cent of their shots?

    a. 20   b. 25   c. 30   d. 35

36. Which player has the highest ratio of number of shots made to number of shots attempted?

    e. Lyons   f. Allen   g. Jones   h. Olson

37. If Allen had taken as many shots as Jones and maintained his shooting rate, how many shots would he have made?

    a. 13   b. 12   c. 11   d. 10

Mathematics Test   Part A measures specifically the content of high school mathematics courses, emphasizing elementary algebra and geometry as usually taught in grades 9 and 10. Part A may be used independently of Part B. A sample question for this section is as follows.

[3]Reproduced from *Stanford Achievement Test, High School Battery* (New York: Harcourt, Brace & World, Inc., © 1965), by permission of the publisher.

29. Which of the following illustrates a correct theorem?

a.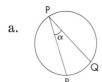

Given: PQ and PR are chords
Therefore: $\sphericalangle\alpha$ = arc RQ (in degrees)

b.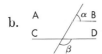

Given: $AB \parallel CD$
Therefore: $\sphericalangle\alpha = \sphericalangle\beta$ (in degrees)

c.

Given: $ABCD$ is an inscribed quadrilateral
Therefore: Area of the circle
$= 2\pi \times$ area of the rectangle $ABCD$

d.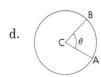

Given: BC and AC are radii
Therefore: $\sphericalangle\theta$ = arc AB (in degrees)

Part B covers more advanced instruction such as advanced algebra, trigonometry, and certain of the newer math concepts.

67. The sample space shown represents the possible outcome of tossing 1 dime and 1 nickel:

● dime—heads
nickel—heads

● dime—heads
nickel—tails

● dime—tails
nickel—heads

● dime—tails
nickel—tails

If we indicate the event A as follows,

● dime—heads
nickel—heads

● dime—heads
nickel—tails ← Event A

● dime—tails
nickel—heads

● dime—tails
nickel—tails

then the event A could be described as _____
   a. the nickel comes up either heads or tails.
   b. the dime comes up heads.
   c. the nickel comes up tails.
   d. the dime comes up heads before the nickel comes up tails.

Science Test   The test questions of this subtest are designed to test science generalizations and their application.

35.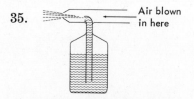

This spray gun works because _____
1. the faster the flow, the lower the pressure of a fluid.
2. greater pressure is caused by thicker liquids.
3. pressure varies inversely with temperature.
4. the greater the depth of a fluid, the higher its pressure.

Social Studies   This test measures knowledge of and the ability to reason in the area of social studies, and assesses social studies skills which are required for further learning in the subject.

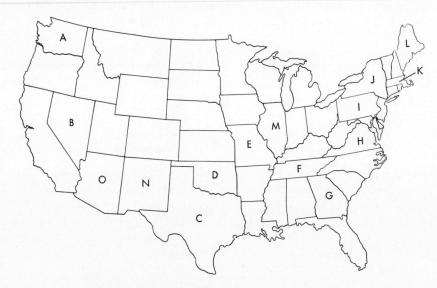

51. Which state was the scene of a famous battle which led to the Mexican War?

   1. State C   2. State D   3. State N   4. State O

52. Gold and silver were discovered in which state in 1859?

   5. State A   6. State B   7. State C   8. State D

English Test   The English subtest is presented in three parts (A, B, and C). Part A measures capitalization, grammar, punctuation, and functional spelling in paragraphs. In Part B, the student is asked to choose from among several compound or complex sentences the one that "expresses the idea best." Part C measures the student's competence in paragraph organization. An example of an item in Part B follows.

53.   1. Because they are so fantastic, only a fool could actually believe the stories Jim tells.
   2. Only a fool could actually believe the fantastic stories which Jim tells.
   3. The stories which Jim tells are so fantastic, actually, but only a fool could believe them.
   4. Being so fantastic, the stories, which Jim tells, only a fool could actually believe them.

Spelling   The spelling subtest covers 240 words in groups of four words each, one of which is misspelled. The misspellings are constructed to represent the common misspellings of students and to reflect generalizations in English spelling.

1.   1. particle   3. eligible
   2. forfiet   4. possible

2.   5. scarcly   7. imitation
   6. afterwards   8. materially

3.   1. examined   3. tremendious
   2. coarse   4. overalls

Arts and Humanities   This test measures the area of classical and contemporary literature, music, art, drama, and philosophy. These areas are represented in the high school curriculum in various subjects or are included as specific teaching in units of other subjects.

53–56. *First read the following passage. Then answer questions 53–56, all of which are concerned with this passage.*

Fanciful poetry and music, used with moderation, are good; but men who are wholly given over to either of them, are commonly as full of whimsies as diseased and splenetic men can be. The true poet is a man who, being conversant in the philosophy of Plato, as it is now accommodated to Christian use (for, as Virgil gives us to understand by his example, that is the only proper, of all other, for an epic poem), who, to his natural endowments, of a large invention, a ripe judgment, and a strong memory, has joined the knowledge of the liberal arts and sciences, and particularly moral philosophy, the mathematics, geography, and history, and with all these qualifications is born a poet;

* knows, and can practice the variety of numbers, and is master of the language in which he writes.

53. This statement suggests at least the following ideas: (1) poetic inspiration by itself is of only slight value, (2) the poet must be learned and must discipline himself carefully, (3) the examples set by the ancient writers should be followed. These ideas are typical of the artistic and intellectual movement known as _____

1. imagism.   3. avant-gardism.
2. existentialism.   4. neoclassicism.

54. In literature, references such as these to Plato and Virgil are called _____

5. allusions.   7. metaphors.
6. illusions.   8. pedantries.

55. The word "numbers" in line 14(*) refers to _____
1. musical chords.
2. basic philosophical considerations.
3. the science of verse rhythms.
4. arithmetic.

56. The group of poets and writers most opposed to the ideas suggested in this passage would be the _____

5. classicists.   7. romantics.
6. Edwardians.   8. humanists.

Technical Comprehension   This subtest is designed to serve both as a general test in the field of industrial arts and as a measure of technical comprehension and applied science for the educated citizen.

(Use the electronic circuit drawing below in answering questions 39–42.)

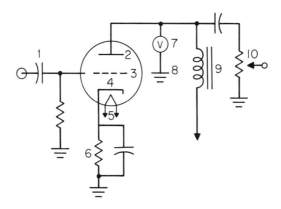

In the above partially complete electronic circuit, identify the following parts according to their designating numbers in the circuit diagram.

39. Potentiometer (variable resistance)

    a. 10   b. 6   c. 8   d. not shown

40. Speaker coil

    e. 1   f. not shown   g. 8   h. 7

41. Ammeter

    a. 3   b. 9   c. 10   d. not shown

42. Antenna

    e. 1   f. not shown   g. 2   h. 10

Business and Economics   This test is designed to serve two functions: (1) as a general test in the field of business education, and (2) as a measure of business and economics for the educated citizen. The test covers various aspects of investments, insurance, taxes, advertising, recordkeeping, real estate, accounting, installment buying, banking procedures, business law, and business writing.

35. The office of Hamilton Company maintains a folder for Arthur C. Case. The file clerk in the office of Hamilton Company should place a carbon copy of a letter addressed to Mr. Case on November 18, 1964 _____

    a. immediately behind the carbon copy of a letter to Mr. Case dated November 14, 1964.
    b. immediately behind the most recent letter from Mr. Case, which is dated November 10, 1964.
    c. immediately behind a letter from Mr. Case dated November 16, 1964 (the most recent communication from him).
    d. immediately in front of a letter from Mr. Case dated November 16, 1964 (the most recent communication from him).

60. John H. Bakmann is preparing a deposit ticket of cash items to be credited to his account at the First National Bank in Wichita, Kansas. Among these cash items are 25 checks. Fifteen are on banks in Wichita; 5 on banks in other cities in Kansas; and 5 on out-of-state banks. Each check should be properly identified on the deposit ticket by _____

    e. its date.
    f. Mr. Bakmann's name.
    g. its A.B.A. number.
    h. Mr. Bakmann's social security number.

STUDENT MOTIVATION FOR TAKING PUBLISHED TESTS

An important area that is often neglected in discussions of the use of published test scores in the schools deals with the motivation of the student for taking a test of this nature. Sears, in his discussion of motivational factors in aptitude testing, provides a theoretical framework of the problem.[4]

> Behavior can be said to be dependent on "ability" and "motivation." To state this idea in somewhat less vague terms, one can say: What actually is done by the individual at a given time depends partly on the "possibilities" inherent in the person and in the situation, partly on the

---

[4]R. Sears, "Motivational Factors in Aptitude Testing," *American Journal of Ortho-psychiatry*, 13 (1943), 492.

forces (drives, goals) acting upon the person at the time. . . the subject should be comfortable emotionally and readily accept the goals required in the different tasks of the test.

Goldman devotes a complete chapter in his book to the psychological and mechanical aspects of test administration.[5] He warns that it is all too easy to regard the actual taking and scoring of tests as a simple, mechanical process when, in fact, the taking of a test by a student "taps a myriad of attitudes, feelings, wishes, needs, abilities, interests, and all the relevant experiences that he has ever had."

During the last 15 years, publishers of tests have begun to acknowledge the significance of motivation on the validity of test scores. In 1959, the authors of the textbook, *Measurement for Guidance*, pointed out that since the motivation of the test taker is so important, one would think that test authors and publishers would do more with regard to presenting material prior to the test which would prepare the students for taking the tests.[6] They present examples of test instructions typical of the perfunctory manner in which students are given tests; e.g., "As soon as booklets and pencils are distributed say: 'Fill in the blanks on the cover, but do not open the booklets. This is a test to see what you can do with your hands and eyes. Use the pencils provided.' " The authors suggest that meaningful material be read to the students regarding the purposes of the tests and how they can be helpful to the student.

Test publishers have made an effort to improve the instructions given to the students by the test administrator. The *Iowa Tests of Educational Development*, for example, are now preceded by a lengthy paragraph to be read to the students which explains the importance of taking the tests and what the results can mean to them.[7]

Educators seem to agree that motivation continues to be a significant factor in the validity of test scores, and that there is an urgency for improving this validity because of the increased use of tests for evaluating educational systems. Swan and Hop-

[5]L. Goldman, *Using Tests in Counseling* (New York: Appleton-Century-Crofts, 1961), p. 95.
[6]J. W. Rothney, P. J. Danielson, and R. A. Hiemann, *Measurement for Guidance* (New York: Harper & Row, Publishers, 1959), p. 97.
[7]Science Research Associates, *The Iowa Tests of Educational Development, Manual for the School Administrator* (Chicago: Science Research Associates, Inc., 1963).

kins express their concern over the fact that test authors assume that a student taking a standardized test will be "trying to do his best," while educators know this assumption often does not hold true. Some students do not even finish; others find the test such a failing and frustrating situation that they dispatch the agony as quickly as possible by filling out the answer sheet without opening the test booklet.[8]

An approach to the problem of motivating students for taking tests is offered by Goldman.[9] He suggests that individuals who have little appreciation of the possible value of tests for later counseling, and who take tests with an attitude not conducive to accurate measurement, may perceive the testing program more realistically if adequate pretest preparation is given. Through either individual or group meetings prior to the testing session, the students should be given the opportunity of becoming active participants in planning for and understanding the purposes of the testing program. He states that many institutions, aware of the shortcomings of mass testing programs, have atempted to improve student motivation and decrease undue anxiety by use of group orientation meetings prior to testing.

If most students in the secondary schools are required to take standardized tests periodically throughout their school years, and school personnel desire the most valid test results upon which to base their educational decisions, teachers should be cognizant of the need to reduce the apparent antitest sentiment shown by numbers of students. This will in turn increase their motivational level and provide more valid test results.

TELLING PARENTS ABOUT TEST SCORES

This section is not concerned with *whether* parents should be told about their children's standardized achievement or intelligence test results, but *how* and *how much* they should be told. Parents have a right to know whatever the school knows about the abilities, the achievement level, and the problems of their children, and the school has the obligation to communicate understandable and usable knowledge.

Few educators will disagree that parents have the final re-

[8]R. Swan and K. Hopkins, "An Investigation of Theoretical and Empirical Chance Scores on Selected Standardized Group Tests," *California Journal of Educational Research*, 16 (1965), 34–41.

[9]Goldman, *loc. cit.*

sponsibility for the upbringing and education of their children. Because of this, all pertinent information bearing on educational and vocational decisions should be made available to the parents and their children. Responsible parents do not take these responsibilities lightly.

The parents' right to know, then, can be regarded as indisputable. But how and how much should parents be told?

A distinction should be made between intelligence tests and achievement tests when deciding how and how much should be reported to parents. Many school personnel who would hesitate to report intelligence test results to parents see no reason why achievement test results should not be shared with them. This is because measures of intelligence are erroneously considered by many school personnel to indicate something quite fixed and final, while achievement scores offer a much greater opportunity for parents (and students) to take a realistic look at the ability picture.

The most generally accepted classification of various IQ levels is based on the 1960 revision of the Stanford-Binet Intelligence Scale.[10] The limits for each of the classifications, however, should not be considered exact.

Classification of IQ Levels

Classification	*IQ*
Very Superior	140 and above
Superior	120 to 139
High Average	110 to 119
Normal Average	90 to 109
Low Average	80 to 89
Borderline Defective	70 to 79
Mentally Defective	69 and below

Achievement   Probably the most common way to interpret the results of a standardized achievement test to junior and senior high school students is by using *percentile scores*. If percentile scores are used, their two essential characteristics should be made clear. First, they refer not to per cent of questions answered correctly, but to per cent of people whose performance the student equalled or surpassed. Second, the student is being compared with a specific group of people. The second point re-

[10]L. M. Terman and M. A. Merrill, *Stanford-Binet Intelligence Scale* (Boston: Houghton Mifflin Company, 1960), p. 18.

quires a definite description of the comparison or norm group in order for the test results to be meaningful. In other words, is the student being compared to a national sample, the local school, or a classroom group? Therefore, a percentile indicates the position of a student within a defined group. It states the extent to which he deviates from the average—the fiftieth percentile.

Another basic type of score used in the elementary and junior high school that interprets the individual score by placing it in comparison with the average score of a defined group is the *grade equivalent*. Using the grade equivalent, the individual score is interpreted by saying it approximates the average score at a given grade.

Grade equivalents are found by computing the mean raw score obtained by students in each grade. For example, if the average number of problems solved correctly in the eighth grade is 62, then the raw score of 62 corresponds to a grade equivalent of eight. Intervening grade equivalents, indicating fractions of a grade, are expressed by decimals. Because the school year covers ten months, each of these months can be expressed as decimals. To illustrate, 8.0 refers to average performance at the beginning of the eighth grade (September testing), 8.5 refers to average performance at the middle of the grade (February testing), and 8.9 is the average performance at the end of the grade (June testing).

Grade equivalents seem so straightforward and simple that serious misunderstanding may result from their use. As noted in a pamphlet,[11] a sixth-grade student with grade equivalent scores of 10.0 for reading and 8.5 in arithmetic does not necessarily rank higher in reading than he does in arithmetic when compared to other sixth graders. Both scores may be at the ninety-fifth percentile for his class, but arithmetic progress, much more than reading, tends to be dependent upon what has been taught, and thus spreads over a narrower range at any one grade.

If a school decides to report grade equivalents, some gross way of expressing a student's standing in relation to a national average should be worked out. One possible way is as follows: *average* for grade equivalents between one-half year below the norm and one-half year above the norm; *good* for grade equivalents

[11]M. R. Katz, *Selecting an Achievement Test* (Princeton, N.J.: Educational Testing Service, E and A Series, No. 3, 1958), p. 26.

in the range from one-half year above the norm to one and one-half years above the norm; *superior* for grade equivalents which exceed the norm by more than one and one-half years; *poor* and *low* might be used for comparable ranges below the average classification.

Another type of score that is used to interpret test results to parents and students in the secondary schools is the *stanine*. Scores are expressed along a scale ranging from one (low) to nine (high), with the value five always representing average performance for students in the comparison or norm group. The percentages of students at each stanine level are shown in the table.

A particularly useful feature of stanines is that they are equally spaced units in a scale, i.e., a stanine of eight is as much better than a stanine of six as a stanine of five is better than a three. Therefore, students' achievement in various tested areas, as expressed in stanine terms, is an accurate illustration of relative strengths and weaknesses.

Stanines indicate a student's standing in a subject in comparison with other students in his same grade placement. A student of stanine seven, eight, or nine is well above the typical student in his grade in the subject measured, while the student in stanine one, two, or three is definitely below.

Percentages of Students and Qualitative Meaning for Each Stanine Level

Stanine	*Percentages of Students*	*Qualitative Meaning*
9	4%	superior (4%)
8	7%	above
7	12%	average (19%)
6	17%	average
5	20%	(54%)
4	17%	.
3	12%	below
2	7%	average (19%)
1	4%	poor (4%)

The nine levels of achievement into which students may be grouped according to the stanine system constitute as fine a classification as the teacher can ordinarily use for appraisal of the individual student's strengths or weaknesses.

Realtionship between Intelligence and Achievement   Generally, it is well for teachers to point out to parents what might be the normal expected achievement for that student's ability level. Teachers and parents should understand clearly that the achievement norm is not a realistic standard for all students; it represents the average achievement of students of average intelligence who have had normal school instruction. In using norms for individual students, or for groups, account must be taken of any deviations from the average situation, particularly as to intelligence. The teacher who exerts terrific effort to bring "all his students up to the norm" lacks this understanding. Usually there will be some who, because of limited ability, should never be pressed to reach this goal, and there will be others who would not be using their full capabilities if they did not greatly exceed the achievement norms for their grade placements. Reporting to parents should always include this interpretation of achievement in relation to intelligence.

SUMMARY STATEMENT

Standardized tests have been spoken of as a "necessary evil"; however, they are not necessarily evil. Misused and misunderstood, they can be a real menace. But they should be considered a blessing to education. Teachers, counselors, and educational administrators need to be certain about what tests can and cannot do before they use them. Then they can use the results to improve education for all.

SUGGESTED READINGS

Anastasi, A., *Psychological Testing* (3rd ed.). New York: The Macmillan Company, 1968. This book is well written, logically constructed, and extremely thorough in its coverage of both basic principles and the vast array of psychological and educational tests available.

Cronbach, L. J., *Essentials of Psychological Testing* (2nd ed.). New York: Harper & Row, Publishers, 1960. This book presents the principles of testing in such a way that the student will learn how to choose tests wisely for particular needs, and will be aware of the potentialities and limitations of the tests he chooses.

Goldman, L., *Using Tests in Counseling*. New York: Appleton-Century-Crofts, 1961. This book explores thoroughly the various ways test results can be interpreted in a school situation. The author covers both theoretical ways as well as researched attempts to develop competency in the interpretation of test results.

Horrocks, J. E., *Assessment of Behavior*. Columbus, Ohio: Charles E. Merrill Books, Inc., 1964. This book devotes chapters to the nature and meaning of intelligence, special ability, and personality. The author also discusses maturation and readiness, achievement, social behavior, and interests and attitudes.

Jackson, D. N., and S. Messick, eds., *Problems in Human Assessment*. New York: McGraw-Hill Book Company, 1967. This is a book of readings dealing, among other things, with the assessment of intellectual abilities, the discovery and encouragement of exceptional talent, and the nature and nurture of creative talent.

Nunnally, J. C., *Psychometric Theory*. New York: McGraw-Hill Book Company, 1967. This book presents a complete picture of the major issues in psychometric theory, including: the logic of psychological measurement, scaling models that underlie particular kinds of measures, and detailed methods for the construction and validation of measures.

Pinneau, S. R., *Changes in Intelligence Quotient*. Boston: Houghton Mifflin Company, 1961. A comprehensive study dealing with the consistency of the intelligence quotient, accurate mental age scores, IQ changes with age, and the rate of mental maturation by subjects of different levels of ability.

Thorndike, R. L., and E. Hagen, *Measurement and Evaluation in Psychology and Education* (2nd ed). New York: John Wiley & Sons, Inc., 1962, Chaps. 9 and 11. An excellent discussion covering the nature and uses of intelligence and achievement tests in the schools.

11

A Look into the Future

Exciting breakthroughs toward improved instruction are being created by the recent development of such new technological devices as instructional television, programmed instruction, computer-assisted instruction, self-instruction, listening laboratories, and tele-lectures, which are being used in numerous schools throughout the country. With their increased instructional use, the secondary teacher should be aware of the potential offered by each of these devices for improving his appraisal of student achievement.

This chapter will discuss the measurement of learning outcomes when new technological devices are used, present a brief description of the instructional uses of each, and indicate some of the potential evaluation possibilities when using these devices.

MEASUREMENT OF LEARNING OUTCOMES

Evaluation of the effectiveness of a secondary school instructional program in which new technological de-

144

vices are used raises a number of questions different from the ones that have been discussed earlier about the measurement of student achievement. As is true of all instructional programs, student knowledge of subject matter is only one of several behavioral outcomes that might be considered. This discussion will be limited to the measurement of subject-matter skill and knowledge. Achievement measurement may therefore be defined as the assessment of criterion behavior, i.e., adequacy of the student's performance with respect to specified standards. When used in this context, the term "criterion" does not necessarily refer to end-of-course performance. Rather, criterion levels may be set up at any point in the instructional sequence when you feel it is necessary to obtain information as to the adequacy of the student's performance.

It is important to distinguish among the student's *entering*, *auxiliary*, and *terminal* behaviors when using technological devices in the instructional sequence. Entering behaviors are those with which a student *comes* to the instructional situation; auxiliary behaviors are those *caused* by the instructional procedures and used in reaching desired educational goals; and terminal behaviors are those *final* sets of behaviors with which a student is expected to leave the learning situation.

The importance of obtaining a measurement of the student's abilities prior to instruction must be stressed. It cannot be assumed that students in any classroom are roughly comparable in aptitude, achievement, and background. Since an instructional sequence using technological devices is geared to the individual, the level at which the "program" begins is critical and must be based on careful assessment of each student's entering behavior.

In the case of auxiliary behaviors, the process of reaching an educational objective is facilitated by determining for each of the steps of the "program" the subject-matter stimuli to which the learner responds, and the kinds of responses each step requires. These activities are usually overt and provide the teacher with necessary information on the learner's progress through the instructional sequence.

Terminal behaviors are, by definition, the educational goals of the instructional sequence. The first step in determining their nature is to have the teacher define the kinds of behaviors (perhaps test performance) which should be shown by the student as proof that he understands the course material. Once these behaviors have been identified it becomes necessary to determine what combination of educational experiences (small group discussions, films, instructional television, and so on) will produce this desired result.

Evaluation instruments used in this type of instructional program should be clearly and specifically based on the objectives of instruction. The criterion objectives defined in the course outline become topics to be covered in the course. These outlines are used as reference points when writing test items, and the teacher should specify the minimum level of performance that each student should have before going on to the next course or unit in a sequence. These criterion-referenced measures become justifiable "proficiency exams" for the instructional unit.

EVALUATION OF STUDENT ACHIEVEMENT WHEN USING NEW TECHNOLOGICAL DEVICES

The technological devices discussed in this section are used in many schools to supplement the teacher's classroom responsibilities. There are no indications that the teaching task is being taken over by these devices. Instead, they are primarily used as part of a large number of teaching techniques. The primary purpose of these devices is the improvement of instruction and enhancement of the teacher-student relationship.

The following brief descriptions are intended merely to stimulate your thinking about innovative ways these technological devices can assist you in the appraisal of student achievement.

Instructional Television   This term describes the use of television for direct, formal instruction regardless of age or grade, whether or not the course is given for credit, and for in-school instruction in various parts of courses, either for direct teaching or for facilitating lecture-demonstrations.

Some of the most interesting uses of television are those enabling a teacher to present and students to observe events that would otherwise be inaccessible or unobservable, or in which the presence of observers would be distracting to the events under study. For example, a demonstration of a lathe in operation, with emphasis on safety rules in its use, could be presented in a course in industrial arts. Student knowledge of these safety rules can then be assessed either by a paper and pencil test, or, if a videotape is used, can be evaluated during a reshowing of the sequence by stopping the tape at predetermined times and asking for student responses to pertinent questions.

Students are also able to observe job interviews and become acquainted with the procedures used in conducting them. Once again, if videotape is used, these same events may be role-played by the students and played back for student and teacher evaluation. After a period of training, the students may again role-play a job interview and be evaluated in terms of progress made.

In the area of physical education, the use of a television system, i.e., camera, videotape recorder, and monitor, offers the teacher many possibilities of evaluating student achievement. In golf, taping a practice session allows the student to see, criticize, repeat, and improve his own performance. The student's rate of improvement at various stages during the instructional sequence can be evaluated.

Listening Laboratories   The listening laboratory, as it is usually called in most schools, is a facility for the study of foreign languages. It is self-contained suite, including a control room, a recording studio, and a classroom. The classroom contains, typically, from 20 to 60 student stations, each equipped with a tape recorder which is capable of duplicating, playing back, recording or listening, and audio-lingual testing. The teacher's console allows for recording of student responses, instructions to one or to all student stations, and dissemination of several different exercises to different student stations simultaneously. Many foreign language teachers are well-prepared to operate this system optimally, including the measurement of student achievement in understanding and speaking the foreign language.

A different use of this facility might be for a biology teacher to require his students to study an assigned chapter or article, and then discuss, by use of previously recorded questions on an audiotape, the students' reactions to the assignment. The teacher need not be present during this discussion. Later, the teacher could listen to the tapes and make notes of points the students overlooked or which are in need of clarification. In later class sessions he would cover these specific points. In effect, this process serves as an oral pretest, allowing the teacher to emphasize in his class discussions those topics which his students do not fully understand.

Another example of the functional use of audiotapes involves the speech teacher who has his students record their speeches on one track of a dual-track tape, while he sits in the back of the room with a microphone and records his comments on the second track as the speech is delivered. The teacher's comments to the class at the conclusion of the speech are also recorded. The student then listens to a stereo replay of the tape as soon as possible and as often as necessary. This replay enables the student to hear his own speech and the teacher's comments on it simultaneously.

Programmed Instruction   Programmed instruction is a technique of self-instruction that presents instructional material in small segments, followed by a task that permits the student to demonstrate his comprehension or skill. If he performs the task correctly, he is presented with another sequence to learn; if he makes a mistake, he must either restudy the same material or "branch" to additional instruction before being allowed to proceed with the next sequence. These programs are constructed in such a manner that they provide the student taking them with information as to whether the response he makes is correct or incorrect. The reinforcement effect of immediate knowledge of success or failure has been found to be a powerful stimulus to learning. Immediate knowledge of an incorrect answer tends to extinguish the incorrect response. Conversely, an immediately rewarded correct answer tends to be reinforced to the point where it is likely to be repeated on the next occasion.

Programmed instructional materials provide teachers and students with several important advantages, such as furnishing means of supplemental instruction, permitting students to catch up, and motivating the work of students especially interested in learning through this medium. Suitable examinations can be developed to assess the student's attainment of knowledge and skills at any time during the program or at the end of a unit of study.

Computer-assisted Instruction   The use of computers in the secondary schools appears to be quite rare and largely in the experimental stage. Most of the activity in this area in the public schools is usually under the direction of college or university faculty researchers.

Perhaps the most widespread instructional use of computers at the present time is in connection with scoring classroom exams or standardized tests. The computer has several significant advantages in correcting and analyzing examination results. It provides the teacher and the student with almost instantaneous reports of the student's total performance on an exam, thus allowing the teacher the opportunity to adapt his later presentations to meet any inadequacies revealed by these data. In addition, computers can provide detailed diagnostic reports on the performance of individual students, enabling the teacher to make individual assignment of study activity for each student. Test questions can also be evaluated and improved in a similar way after it is known what proportion of students in the upper and lower areas of the distribution answered the items correctly.

An active and outstanding example of computer-assisted instruction making use of dialogue between a student and the computer is the PLATO (Programmed Logic for Automatic Teaching Operations) project at the University of Illinois at Urbana.[1] The student console used with this system consists of a typewriter connected to a computer with a small electronic screen. The student communicates with the computer by using one of a series of command keys, or by typing answers to problems presented by the computer and appearing on the screen. The screen can display information from two sources: (1) a programmed series of slides, with random access as needed by each student; or (2) an electronic blackboard that will show instructions printed out by the computer, responses typed by the student, and reactions of the computer to the correctness of the student responses.

Self-instruction   The self-instruction laboratory provides the space and the materials necessary for each student to learn at his own rate the concepts and information or skills for a given course. A distinguishing feature of the self-instructional center is that a student ordinarily (but not always) attends self-study sessions on his own, not by assignment. In other words, the school furnishes the equipment and materials needed for the presentation (the opportunity), but the student must supply the motivation.

A common application of the self-instruction center is one that enables the student to catch up on missed work or to supplement class materials by listening or working through a printed instructional program, in much the same manner as students have always studied in the library. The teacher arranges for these materials, e.g., class assignment sheets, tapes of valuable discussions taken from radio or television, printed programmed books, and so on, to be available to the student on his request. The self-instructional activity is usually supplemented by periodic teacher-student conferences to discuss the materials covered and answer

[1] J. W. Brown and J. W. Thornton, eds., *New Media in Higher Education* (Washington, D.C.: National Education Association, 1963).

any questions that the student may have. Evaluation of student attainment of the knowledge or skills necessary to go on to another sequence of study may be made in the self-instructional center or during the periodic meetings with the student.

Tele-lecture   Tele-lecture is simply a lecture via telephone. Many high schools have made excellent use of this technique to profit from instructional contributions of guests who cannot come to the school. State political leaders, scientists, or college specialists may find it impossible to travel to a particular high school or group of schools, but quite possible and satisfactory to sit at a telephone and be interviewed for instructional purposes.

A somewhat different use of the tele-lecture involves having an authority present a lecture to students in a group of schools in a city. Rooms in the schools can be equipped with the equipment necessary to allow for proper amplification and transmission of student questions. When the lecture is scheduled in advance, any necessary charts, slides, or other types of materials may be sent prior to the lecture. It has been found that taping the lecture is a good practice in order to allow other student groups the opportunity to hear it in the future. In such cases, the "live" listeners may ask questions, and all listeners in the network are able to hear the questions and answers.

Evaluation of student achievement using this instructional approach may take many forms, a few of which would include the following: (1) have the students write an essay covering certain major points presented in the lecture that are most relevant to the teacher's course objectives; (2) evaluate the students' comments in regard to understanding and application of the presentation to their own community; or (3) replay the tape of the lecture, stop it at predetermined spots and ask the students to write their responses to specific questions, and then start the tape again. This would allow almost immediate reinforcement to the students concerning the correctness of their answers.

SUMMARY STATEMENT

The instructional uses of these technological devices will, in future years, increase in schools throughout the country. The teacher should bear in mind that these devices possess no magic. The key to better evaluation of student achievement, now as in the future, is the teacher.

SUGGESTED READINGS

Ausubel, D. P., "The Use of Advance Organizers in the Learning and Retention of Meaningful Verbal Material," *Journal of Educational Psychology*, 51 (October 1960), 267–272.

Brish, W. M., "Washington County Closed Circuit Television Report," *AV Communications Review*, 13 (Summer 1965), 228.

Bundy, R. F., "Computer-Assisted Instruction: Now and the Future," *Audio-Visual Instruction*, 12 (April 1967), 344–348.

Coulson, L. E., and H. F. Siberman, "Automated Teaching and Individual Differences," *AV Communications Review*, 9 (January-February 1961), 4–15.

Eigen, L. D., "High School Students' Reactions to Programmed Instruction," *AV Communications Review*, 14 (Summer 1966), 275.

Gagne, R. M., "The Acquisition of Knowledge," *Psychological Review*, 69 (July 1962), 355–365.

Keating, R. F., "A Study of the Effectiveness of Language Laboratories," *AV Communications Review*, 12 (Spring 1964), 106–107.

Lange, P. C., ed., *National Society for the Study of Education: Programmed Instruction*, Sixty-Sixth Yearbook, Part II. Chicago: University of Chicago Press, 1967, p. 334.

Lublin, S. C., "Reinforcement Schedules, Scholastic Aptitude, Autonomy Need, and Achievement in a Programmed Course," *Journal of Educational Psychology*, 56 (December 1965), 295–302.

Pressey, S. L., "A Simple Device for Teaching, Testing, and Research in Learning," *School and Society*, 23 (1926), 373–376.

Schramm, W. S., *Research on Programmed Instruction: An Annotated Bibliography*. Washington, D.C.: U.S. Government Printing Office, 1964, p. 114.

Skinner, B. F., "Teaching Machines," *Science*, 128 (October 1958), 969–977.

———, *The Technology of Teaching*. New York: Appleton-Century-Crofts, 1968, p. 271.

Appendix I:

A Glossary of

Measurement Terms[1]

This glossary of technical terms used in educational and psychological measurement is primarily for persons with limited training in measurement, rather than for the specialist. The terms defined are the most common or basic ones such as occur in test manuals and simple research reports.

The definitions are based on study of the definitions and usages of the various terms in about a dozen widely used textbooks in educational and psychological measurement and statistics, and in both general and specialized dictionaries. There is not complete uniformity among writers in the measurement field with respect to the usage of certain technical terms; in case of varying usage, either these variations are noted or the definition offered is the one that the writer judges to represent the "best" usage.

[1]Reproduced from R. T. Lennon, *et al.*, "A Glossary of 100 Measurement Terms," *Test Service Notebook No. 13* (New York: Harcourt, Brace & World, Inc., © 1957), by permission of the publisher.

Academic aptitude. The combination of native and acquired abilities that is needed for school work; likelihood of success in mastering academic work, as estimated from measures of the necessary abilities. (Also called *scholastic aptitude.*)

Accomplishment quotient (AQ). The ratio of educational age to mental age; EA ÷ MA. (Also called *achievement quotient.*)

Achievement age. The age for which a given achievement test score is the real or estimated average. (Also called *educational age* or *subject age.*) If the achievement age corresponding to a score of 36 on a reading test is 10 years, 7 months (10–7), this means that pupils 10 years, 7 months achieve, on the average, a score of 36 on the test.

Achievement test. A test that measures the extent to which a person has "achieved" something—acquired certain information or mastered certain skills, usually as a result of specific instruction.

Age equivalent. The age for which a given score is the real or estimated average score.

Age norms. Values representing typical or average performance for persons of various age groups.

Age-grade table. A table showing the number or per cent of pupils of various ages in each grade; a distribution of the ages of pupils in successive grades.

Alternate-form reliability. The closeness of correspondence, or correlation, between results on alternate (i.e., equivalent or parallel) forms of a test; thus, a measure of the extent to which the two forms are consistent or reliable in measuring whatever they do measure, assuming that the examinees themselves do not change in the abilities measured between the two testings. (See *reliability, reliability coefficient, standard error.*)

Aptitude. A combination of abilities and other characteristics, whether native or acquired, known or believed to be indicative of an individual's ability to learn in some particular area. Thus, "musical aptitude" would refer broadly to that combination of physical and mental characteristics, motivational factors, and conceivably other characteristics which is conducive to acquiring proficiency in the musical field. Some exclude motivational factors, including interests, from the concept of "aptitude," but the more comprehensive use seems preferable. The layman may think of "aptitude" as referring only to some inborn capacity; the term is no longer so restricted in its psychological or measurement usage.

Arithmetic mean.   The sum of a set of scores divided by the number of scores. (Commonly called *average*, mean.)

Average.   A general term applied to measures of central tendency. The three most widely used averages are the *arithmetic mean*, the *median*, and the *mode*.

Battery.   A group of several tests standardized on the same population, so that results on the several tests are comparable. Sometimes loosely applied to any group of tests administered together, even though not standardized on the same subjects.

Ceiling.   The upper limit of ability measured by a test.

Class analysis chart.   A chart, usually prepared in connection with a battery of achievement tests, that shows the relative performance of members of a class on the several parts of the battery.

Coefficient of correlation (r).   A measure of the degree of relationship, or "going-togetherness," between two sets of measures for the same group of individuals. The correlation coefficient most frequently used in test development and educational research is that known as the *Pearson (Pearsonian) r*, so named for Karl Pearson, originator of the method, or as the *product-moment r*, to denote the mathematical basis of its calculation. Unless otherwise specified, "correlation" usually means the product-moment correlation coefficient, which ranges from .00, denoting complete absence of relationship, to 1.00, denoting perfect correspondence, and may be either positive or negative.

Completion item.   A test question calling for the completion (filling in) of a phrase, sentence, etc., from which one or more parts have been omitted.

Correction for guessing.   A reduction in score for wrong answers, sometimes applied in scoring true-false or multiple-choice questions. Many question the validity or usefulness of this device, which is intended to discourage guessing and to yield more accurate ranking of examinees in terms of their true knowledge. Scores to which such corrections have been applied—e.g., rights minus wrongs, or rights minus some fraction of wrongs—are often spoken of as "corrected for guessing" or "corrected for chance."

Correlation.   Relationship or "going-togetherness" between two scores or measures; tendency of one score to vary concomitantly with the other, as the tendency of students of high IQ to be above average in reading ability. The existence of a strong relationship—i.e., a high correlation—between two variables does not necessarily indicate that one has any causal influence on the other. (See *coefficient of correlation.*)

Criterion. A standard by which a test may be judged or evaluated; a set of scores, ratings, etc., that a test is designed to predict or to correlate with. (See *validity.*)

Decile. Any one of the nine percentile points (scores) in a distribution that divide the distribution into ten equal parts; every tenth percentile. The first decile is the 10th percentile, the ninth decile the 90th percentile, etc.

Deviation. The amount by which a score differs from some reference value, such as the mean, the norm, or the score on some other test.

Deviation IQ. See *intelligence quotient.*

Diagnostic test. A test used to "diagnose," that is, to locate specific areas of weakness or strength, and to determine the nature of weaknesses or deficiencies; it yields measures of the components or sub-parts of some larger body of information or skill. Diagnostic achievement tests are most commonly prepared for the skill subjects—reading, arithmetic, spelling.

Difficulty value. The per cent of some specified group, such as students of a given age or grade, who answer an item correctly.

Discriminating power. The ability of a test item to differentiate between persons possessing much of some trait and those possessing little.

Distractor. Any of the incorrect choices in a multiple-choice or matching item.

Distribution (frequency distribution). A tabulation of scores from high to low, or low to high, showing the number of individuals that obtain each score or fall in each score interval.

Educational age (EA). See *achievement age.*

Equivalent form. Any of two or more forms of a test that are closely parallel with respect to the nature of the content and the difficulty of items included, and that will yield very similar average scores and measures of variability for a given group.

Error of measurement. See *standard error.*

Extrapolation. In general, any process of estimating values of a function beyond the range of available data. As applied to test norms, the process of extending a norm line beyond the limits of actually obtained data, in order to permit interpretation of extreme scores. This extension may be done mathematically by fitting a curve to the obtained data or, as is more common, by less rigorous methods, usually graphic. See Fig. 1. Considerable judgment on the testmaker's part enters into any extrapolation process, which means that extrapolated norm values are likely to be to some extent arbitrary.

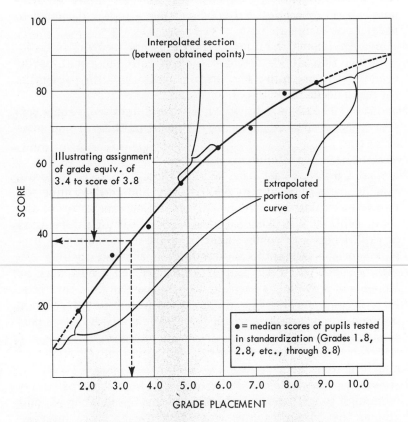

FIGURE 1.   Sample Grade Norm Line, for a Test Standardized in Grades 1 through 8, Illustrating Extrapolation and Interpolation, and Process of Assigning Grade Equivalents.

Factor.   In mental measurement, a hypothetical trait, ability, or component of ability, that underlies and influences performance on two or more tests, and hence causes scores on the tests to be correlated. The term "factor" strictly refers to a theoretical variable, derived by a process of *factor analysis,* from a table of intercorrelations among tests; but it is also commonly used to denote the psychological interpretation given to the variable—i.e., the mental trait assumed to be represented by the variable, as verbal ability, numerical ability, etc.

Factor analysis.   Any of several methods of analyzing the intercorrelations among a set of variables such as test scores. Factor analysis attempts to account for the interrelationships in terms of some underlying "factors," preferably fewer in number than the original variables; and it reveals how much of the variation in each of the original measures arises from, or is associated with, each of the hypothetical factors. Factor analysis has contributed to our understanding of the organization or components of intelligence, aptitudes, and personality; and it has pointed the way to the development of "purer" tests of the several components.

Forced-choice item. Broadly, any multiple-choice item in which the examinee is *required* to select one or more of the given choices. The term is best used to denote a special type of multiple-choice item, in which the options, or choices are (1) of equal "preference value"—i.e., chosen equally often by a typical group, but (2) of differential discriminating ability—i.e., such that one of the options discriminates between persons high and low on the factor that this option measures, while the other options do not.

Frequency distribution. See *distribution.*

Grade equivalent. The grade level for which a given score is the real or estimated average.

Grade norm. The average score obtained by pupils of given grade placement. See *norms, modal age.*

Group test. A test that may be administered to a number of individuals at the same time by one examiner.

Individual test. A test that can be administered to only one person at a time.

Intelligence quotient (IQ). Originally, the ratio of a person's mental age to his chronological age (MA/CA) or, more precisely, especially for older persons, the ratio of mental age to the mental age normal for chronological age (in both cases multiplied by 100 to eliminate the decimal). More generally, IQ is a measure of brightness that takes into account both score on an intelligence test and age. A *deviation IQ* is such a measure of brightness, based on the difference or deviation between a person's obtained score and the score that is normal for the person's age.

The accompanying table shows the classification of IQ's offered by Terman and Merrill for the Stanford-Binet test, indicating the percentage of persons in a normal population who fall in each classification. This table is roughly applicable to tests yielding IQ's having standard deviations of about 16 points (not all do). It is important to bear in mind that any such table is arbitrary, for there are no inflexible lines of demarcation between "feeble-minded" and "borderline," etc.

IQ Classifications of Terman and Merrill
Based on Stanford-Binet Test Results

Classification	IQ	Per Cent of All Persons
Near genius or genius	140 and above	1
Very superior	130–139	2.5
Superior	120–129	8
Above average	110–119	16
Normal or average	90–109	45
Below average	80–89	16
Dull or borderline	70–79	8
Feeble-minded: moron, imbecile, idiot	60–69	2.5
	59 and below	1

Interpolation.   In general, any process of estimating intermediate values between two known points. As applied to test norms, it refers to the procedure used in assigning interpreted values (e.g., grade or age equivalents) to scores between the successive average scores actually obtained in the standardization process. In reading norm tables, it is necessary at times to interpolate to obtain a norm value for a score between scores given in the table; e.g., in the table given here, an age value of 12–5 would be assigned, by interpolation, to a score of 118. See Fig. 1 under *extrapolation*.

Score	Age Equivalent
120	12–6
115	12–4
110	12–2

Inventory test.   As applied to achievement tests, a test that attempts to cover rather thoroughly some relatively small unit of specific instruction or training. The purpose of an inventory test, as the name suggests, is more in the nature of a "stock-taking" of an individual's knowledge or skill than an effort to measure in the usual sense. The term sometimes denotes a type of test used to measure achievement status prior to instruction.

Many personality and interest questionnaires are designated

"inventories," since they appraise an individual's status in several personal characteristics, or his level of interest in a variety of types of activities.

Item. A single question or exercise in a test.

Item analysis. The process of evaluating single test items by any of several methods. It usually involves determining the difficulty value and the discriminating power of the item, and often its correlation with some criterion.

Kuder-Richardson formula(s). Formulas for estimating the reliability of a test from information about the individual items in the test, or from the mean score, standard deviation, and number of items in the test. Because the Kuder-Richardson formulas permit estimation of reliability from a single administration of a test, without the labor involved in dividing the test into halves, their use has become common in test development. The Kuder-Richardson formulas are not appropriate for estimating the reliability of speeded tests.

Machine-scorable (machine-scored) test. A test that may be scored by means of a machine. Ordinarily, the term refers to a test adapted for scoring on the International Test Scoring Machine, manufactured by International Business Machines Corporation. In taking tests that are to be scored on this machine, the examinee records his answers on separate answer sheets with a special electrographic pencil. These pencil marks are electrically conductive, and current flowing through them may be read on a suitably calibrated dial as a test score. The machine distinguishes, by means of appropriate keys, between right and wrong answers, and can combine groups of responses in order to yield total or part scores, weighted scores, or corrected scores.

Matching item. A test item calling for the correct association of each entry in one list with an entry in a second list.

Mean. See *arithmetic mean.*

Median. The middle score in a distribution; the 50th percentile; the point that divides the group into two equal parts. Half of the group of scores fall below the median and half above it.

Mental age (MA). The age for which a given score on an intelligence test is average or normal. If a score of 55 on an intelligence test corresponds to a mental age of 6 years, 10 months, then 55 is presumably the average score that would be made by an unselected group of children 6 years, 10 months of age.

Modal age. That age or age range which is most typical or characteristic of pupils of specified grade placement.

Modal-age norms.   Norms based on the performance of pupils of modal age for their respective grades, which are thus free of the distorting influence of under-age or over-age pupils.

Mode.   The score or value that occurs most frequently in a distribution.

Multiple-choice item.   A test item in which the examinee's task is to choose the correct or best answer from several given answers, or options.

Multiple-response item.   A special type of multiple-choice item in which two or more of the given choices may be correct.

N.   The symbol commonly used to represent the number of cases in a distribution, study, etc.

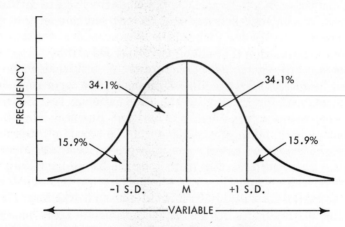

FIGURE 2.   Normal Curve, Showing Areas under the Curve Corresponding to Distances of ±1 Standard Deviation.

Normal distribution.   A distribution of scores or measures that in graphic form has a distinctive bell-shaped appearance. Figure 2 shows such a graph of a normal distribution, known as a normal curve or normal probability curve. In a normal distribution, scores or measures are distributed symmetrically about the mean, with as many cases at various distances above the mean as at equal distances below it, and with cases concentrated near the average and decreasing in frequency the further one departs from the average, according to a precise mathematical equation. The assumption that mental and psychological characteristics are distributed normally has been very useful in much test development work.

Norm line.   A smooth curve drawn through the mean or median scores of successive age or grade groups, or through percentile points for a single group. See Fig. 1 under *extrapolation*.

Norms.   Statistics that describe the test performance of specified groups, such as pupils of various ages or grades in the standardization group for a test. Norms are often assumed to be representative of some larger population, as of pupils in the country as a whole. Norms are descriptive of average, typical, or mediocre performance; they are not to be regarded as standards, or as desirable levels of attainment. Grade, age, and percentile are the most common types of norms.

Objective test.   A test in the scoring of which there is no possibility of difference of opinion among scorers as to whether responses are to be scored right or wrong. It is contrasted with a "subjective" test—e.g., the usual essay examination to which different scorers may assign different scores, ratings, or grades.

Omnibus test.   A test (1) in which items measuring a variety of mental operations are all combined into a single sequence rather than being grouped together by type of operation, and (2) from which only a single score is derived, rather than separate scores for each operation or function. Omnibus tests make for simplicity of administration: one set of directions and one over-all time limit usually suffice. *Otis Quick-Scoring Mental Ability Tests: Beta* or *Gamma Tests* are omnibus-type tests, as distinguished from tests such as *Terman-McNemar Test of Mental Ability* or *Pintner General Ability Tests: Verbal,* in which the items measuring various operations are grouped together, each with its own set of directions.

Percentile (P).   A point (score) in a distribution below which falls the per cent of cases indicated by the given percentile. Thus the 15th percentile denotes the score or point below which 15 per cent of the scores fall. "Percentile" has nothing to do with the per cent of correct answers an examinee has on a test.

Percentile rank.   The per cent of scores in a distribution equal to or lower than the score corresponding to the given rank.

Performance test.   As contrasted with *paper-and-pencil test, a* test requiring motor or manual response on the examinee's part, generally but not always involving manipulation of concrete equipment or materials. *Cornell-Coxe Performance Ability Scale, Arthur Point Scale of Performance Tests,* and *Bennett Hand-Tool Dexterity Test* are performance tests, in this sense. "Performance test" is also used in another sense, to denote a test that is actually a work-sample, and in this sense it may include paper-and-pencil tests, as, for example, a test in accounting, or in taking shorthand, or in proofreading, where no materials other than paper and pencil may be required, but where the test response is identical with the behavior about which information is desired.

Personality test.   A test intended to measure one or more of the non-intellective aspects of an individual's mental or psychological make-up. Personality tests include the so-called *personality inventories* or adjustment inventories (e.g., *Heston Personal Adjustment Inventory, Bernreuter Personality Inventory, Bell Adjustment Inventory*) which seek to measure a person's status on such traits as dominance, sociability, introversion, etc., by means of self-descriptive responses to a series of questions; *rating scales* (e.g., *Haggerty-Olson-Wickman Behavior Rating Schedules*) which call for rating, by one's self or another, of the extent to which a subject possesses certain characteristics; *situation tests* in which the individual's behavior in simulated life-like situations is observed by one or more judges, and evaluated with reference to various personality traits; and *opinion* or *attitude inventories* (e.g., *Allport-Vernon Study of Values*). Some writers also classify interest inventories as personality tests.

Power test.   A test intended to measure level of performance rather than speed of response; hence one in which there is either no time limit or a very generous one.

Practice effect.   The influence of previous experience with a test on a later administration of the same test or a similar test; usually, an increase in the score on the second testing, attributed to increased familiarity with the directions, kinds of questions, etc. Practice effect is greatest when the interval between testings is small, when the materials in the two tests are very similar, and when the initial test-taking represents a relatively novel experience for the subjects.

Probable error.   See *standard error.*

Product-moment coefficient.   See *coefficient of correlation.*

Profile.   A graphic representation of the results on several tests, for either an individual or a group, when the results have been expressed in some uniform or comparable terms. This method of presentation permits easy identification of areas of strength or weakness.

Projective technique (projective method).   A method of personality study in which the subject responds as he chooses to a series of stimuli such as ink-blots, pictures, unfinished sentences, etc. So called because of the assumption that under this free-response condition the subject "projects" into his responses manifestations of personality characteristics and organization that can, by suitable methods, be scored and interpreted to yield a description of his basic personality structure. The *Rorschach* (ink-blot) *Technique* and the Murray *Thematic Apperception Test* are the most commonly used projective methods.

Quartile.   One of three points that divide the cases in a distribution into four equal groups. The lower quartile, or 25th percentile, sets off the lowest fourth of the group; the middle quartile is the same as the 50th percentile, or median; and the third quartile, or 75th percentile, marks off the highest fourth.

r.   See *coefficient of correlation.*

Random sample.   A sample of the members of a population drawn in such a way that every member of the population has an equal chance of being included—that is, drawn in a way that precludes the operation of bias or selection. The purpose in using a sample thus free of bias is, of course, that the sample be fairly "representative" of the total population, so that sample findings may be generalized to the population. A great advantage of random samples is that formulas are available for estimating the expected variation of the sample statistics from their true values in the total population; in other words, we know how precise an estimate of the population value is given by a random sample of any given size.

Range.   The difference between the lowest and highest scores obtained on a test by some group.

Raw score.   The first quantitative result obtained in scoring a test. Usually the number of right answers, number right minus some fraction of number wrong, time required for performance, number of errors, or similar direct, unconverted, uninterpreted measure.

Readiness test.   A test that measures the extent to which an individual has achieved a degree of maturity or acquired certain skills or information needed for undertaking successfully some new learning activity. Thus a *reading readiness test* indicates the extent to which a child has reached a developmental stage where he may profitably begin a formal instructional program in reading.

Recall item.   An item that requires the examinee to supply the correct answer from his own memory or recollection, as contrasted with a *recognition item*, in which he need only identify the correct answer. E.g., "Columbus discovered America in the year ___?___ " is a recall item, whereas "Columbus discovered America in (a) 1425, (b) 1492, (c) 1520, (d) 1546" is a recognition item.

Recognition item.   An item requiring the examinee to recognize or select the correct answer from among two or more given answers. See *recall item*.

Reliability.   The extent to which a test is consistent in measuring whatever it does measure; dependability, stability, relative freedom from errors of measurement. Reliability is usually estimated by some form of *reliability coefficient* or by the *standard error of measurement*.

Reliability coefficient.   The coefficient of correlation between two forms of a test, between scores on repeated administrations of the same test, or between halves of a test, properly corrected. These three coefficients measure somewhat different aspects of reliability but all are properly spoken of as reliability coefficients. See *alternate-form reliability, split-half coefficient, test-retest coefficient, Kuder-Richardson formula(s)*.

Representative sample.   A sample that corresponds to or matches the population of which it is a sample with respect to characteristics important for the purposes under investigation—e.g., in an achievement test norm sample, proportion of pupils from each state, from various regions, from segregated and non-segregated schools, etc.

Scholastic aptitude.   See *academic aptitude*.

Skewness.   The tendency of a distribution to depart from symmetry or balance around the mean.

Sociometry.   Measurement of the interpersonal relationships prevailing among the members of a group. By means of sociometric devices, e.g., the sociogram, an attempt is made to discover the patterns of choice and rejection among the individuals making up the group—which ones are chosen most often as friends or leaders ("stars"), which are rejected by others ("isolates"), how the group subdivides into clusters or cliques, etc.

Spearman-Brown formula.   A formula giving the relationship between the reliability of a test and its length. The formula permits estimation of the reliability of a test lengthened or shortened by any amount, from the known reliability of a test of specified length. Its most common application is in the estimation of reliability of an entire test from the correlation between two halves of the test (*split-half reliability*).

Split-half coefficient. A coefficient of reliability obtained by correlating scores on one half of a test with scores on the other half. Generally, but not necessarily, the two halves consist of the odd-numbered and the even-numbered items.

Standard deviation (S.D.). A measure of the variability or dispersion of a set of scores. The more the scores cluster around the mean, the smaller the standard deviation.

Standard error (S.E.). An estimate of the magnitude of the "error of measurement" in a score—that is, the amount by which an obtained score differs from a hypothetical true score. The standard error is an amount such that in about two-thirds of the cases the obtained score would not differ by more than one standard error from the true score. The *probable error (P.E.)* of a score is a similar measure, except that in about half the cases the obtained score differs from the true score by not more than one probable error. The probable error is equal to about two-thirds of the standard error. The larger the probable or the standard error of a score, the less reliable the measure.

Standard score. A general term referring to any of a variety of "transformed" scores, in terms of which raw scores may be expressed for reasons of convenience, comparability, ease of interpretation, etc. The simplest type of standard score is that which expresses the deviation of an individual's raw score from the average score of his group in relation to the standard deviation of the scores of the group. Thus:

$$\text{Standard score (z)} = \frac{\text{raw score (X)} - \text{mean (M)}}{\text{standard deviation (S.D.)}}$$

By multiplying this ratio by a suitable constant and by adding or subtracting another constant, standard scores having any desired mean and standard deviation may be obtained. Such standard scores do not affect the relative standing of the individuals in the group nor change the shape of the original distribution.

More complicated types of standard scores may yield distributions differing in shape from the original distribution; in fact, they are sometimes used for precisely this purpose. *Normalized standard scores* and *K-scores* (as used in *Stanford Achievement Test*) are examples of this latter group.

Standardized test (standard test). A systematic sample of performance obtained under prescribed conditions, scored according to definite rules, and capable of evaluation by reference to normative information. Some writers restrict the term to tests having the above properties, whose items have been experimentally evaluated, and/or for which evidences of validity and reliability are provided.

Stanine.   One of the steps in a nine-point scale of normalized standard scores. The stanine (short for *standard-nine*) scale has values from 1 to 9, with a mean of 5, and a standard deviation of 2.

Stencil key.   A scoring key which, when positioned over an examinee's responses either in a test booklet or, more commonly, on an answer sheet, permits rapid identification and counting of all right answers. Stencil keys may be perforated in positions corresponding to positions of right answers, so that only right answers show through when the keys are in place; or they may be transparent, with positions of right answers identified by circles, boxes, etc., printed on the key.

Strip key.   A scoring key arranged so that the answers for items on any page or in any column of the test appear in a strip or column that may be placed alongside the examinee's responses for easy scoring.

Survey test.   A test that measures general achievement in a given subject or area, usually with the connotation that the test is intended to measure group status, rather than to yield precise measures of individuals.

Test-retest coefficient.   A type of reliability coefficient obtained by administering the same test a second time after a short interval and correlating the two sets of scores.

True-false item.   A test question or exercise in which the examinee's task is to indicate whether a given statement is true or false.

True score.   A score entirely free of errors of measurement. True scores are hypothetical values never obtained by testing, which always involves some measurement error. A true score is sometimes defined as the average score of an infinite series of measurements with the same or exactly equivalent tests, assuming no practice effect or change in the examinee during the testings.

Validity.   The extent to which a test does the job for which it is used. Validity, thus defined, has different connotations for various kinds of tests and, accordingly, different kinds of validity evidence are appropriate for them. For example:

1. The validity of an achievement test is the extent to which the content of the test represents a balanced and adequate sampling of the outcomes (knowledge, skills, etc.) of the course or instructional program it is intended to cover (*content, face,* or *curricular validity*). It is best evidenced by a comparison of the test content with courses of study, instructional materials, and statements of instructional goals, and by critical analysis of the processes required in responding to the items.

2. The validity of an aptitude, prognostic, or readiness test is the extent to which it accurately indicates future learning success in the area for which it is used as a predictor (*predictive validity*). It is evidenced by correlations between test scores and measures of later success.

3. The validity of a personality test is the extent to which the test yields an accurate description of an individual's personality traits or personality organization (*status validity*). It may be evidenced by agreement between test results and other types of evaluation, such as ratings or clinical classification, but only to the extent that such criteria are themselves valid.

The traditional definition of validity as "the extent to which a test measures what it is supposed to measure," seems less satisfactory than the above, since it fails to emphasize that the validity of a test is always specific to the purposes for which the test is used, and that different kinds of evidence are appropriate for appraising the validity of various types of tests.

Validity of a test *item* refers to the discriminating power of the item—its ability to distinguish between persons having much and those having little of some characteristic.

Appendix II:

Commonly Used Published Tests

GROUP INTELLIGENCE TESTS

California Test of Mental Maturity—Short Form

California Test Bureau
Testing Time: 45 minutes
Grades: 7–9; 9–12

This test is composed of four factors. Factor I, *Logical Reasoning*, presents the examinee with inductive or deductive reasoning problems. Within this major area the following subtests are represented: "similarities," "analogies," and "opposites." Factor II, *Numerical Recall*, involves reasoning in quantitative relationships rather than arithmetical fundamentals. The subtests composing this factor are: "numerical values," and "number problems." Factor III, *Verbal Comprehension*, is determined by using 125 vocabulary words in a variety of formats. Factor IV, *Memory*, is tested by the delayed recall method. That is, the student is queried about stated or implied ideas in a story read to him before the test.

Cooperative School and College Ability Test

Educational Testing Service
Testing Time: 95 minutes
Grades: 6–8; 8–10; 10–12

This test is designed to measure school learned abilities rather than abstract, hard-to-explain psychological traits. It consists of four parts at all levels. These are: *Sentence Understanding, Numerical Computations, Word Meanings,* and *Numerical Problem Solving.* A verbal score is derived from the student's score on Sentence Understanding and Word Meaning Subtests. A quantitative score is derived from the student's performance on Numerical Problem Solving. A total score reflects the student's score on each of the four parts.

Henmon-Nelson Tests of Mental Ability, Revised Edition

Houghton Mifflin Company
Testing Time: 30 minutes
Grades: 6–9; 9–12

Each level of the test contains 90 items arranged in ascending order of difficulty. Types of items include vocabulary, sentence completion, opposites, general information, scrambled letters, scrambled words, verbal inference, number series, arithmetic reasoning, figure analogies, and following directions. The spiral omnibus format of this test presents the tasks in order of difficulty and not by type of item. The test produces one composite score, a deviation IQ.

Kuhlmann-Anderson Intelligence Tests, Seventh Edition

Personnel Press
Testing Time: 30–45 minutes
Grades: 7–9; 9–12

This test is designed to measure those mental characteristics which are important in school learning, and yields three separate scores, i.e., V—verbal, Q—quantitative, and T—total. All three scores can be converted to a percentile rank and, in addition, the total score can be converted to a deviation IQ.

Lorge-Thorndike Intelligence Tests

Houghton Mifflin Company
Testing Time: 65 minutes
Grades: 7–12

This is a series of tests of abstract intelligence. It provides both a Verbal and Nonverbal battery in a single reusable booklet. The verbal battery is made up of five subtests, which are: *Vocabulary, Verbal Classification, Sentence Completion, Arithmetic Reasoning,* and *Verbal Analogy.* The nonverbal battery uses items which are either pictorial or numerical. It contains three subtests: *Pictorial Classification, Pictorial Analogy,* and *Numerical Relationships.* (See Chapter 10 for examples of the test questions used in each subtest.)

Otis-Lennon Mental Ability Test, Advanced Level

Harcourt, Brace & World, Inc.
Testing Time: 40 minutes
Grades: 10–12

This test is designed to measure general mental ability, or scholastic aptitude, of students in American schools. The basic assumptions underlying this instrument are that all students have had substantially equal opportunity to learn the types of things included in the tests, and all students are equally motivated to do their best on a test. Areas measured in this spiral omnibus format include abstract manipulation of ideas expressed in verbal, numerical, figural, or symbolic form.

Otis Quick-Scoring Mental Abilities Tests, New Edition, Gamma

Harcourt, Brace & World, Inc.
Testing Time: 30 minutes
Grades: 9–12

The purpose of this test is to measure the mental ability, that is, the thinking power or the degree of maturity of the mind of the student. The test yields a single score, a deviation IQ, which summarizes the student's performance on 80 items measuring in spiral omnibus format word meaning, verbal analogies, scrambled sentences, interpretation of proverbs, logical reasoning, number series, arithmetic reasoning, and design analogies. More than two-thirds of the 80 items measure some form of verbal competence.

Primary Mental Abilities Test

Science Research Associates
Testing Time: 65–75 minutes
Grades: 9–12

This test is designed to differentiate abilities or aptitudes in five separate scholastic areas. It is also a measure of general intelligence, pertinent to the academic environment. The five scores yielded by this test are: the *total score*, which is a total of the other scores; the *verbal meaning score*, which consists of 60 questions and requires the student to select a synonym for a given word; the *number facility score*, which is obtained from 30 questions which measure the student's speed, use, and understanding of computational skills; the *spatial relations score*, which appraises the student's ability to choose which of the five line figures are rotated in the same plane but otherwise are identical to the given figure; and the *reasoning score*, which measures letter series, word grouping, and number series. There is a very strong emphasis on speed through this test.

GROUP APTITUDE BATTERIES

Academic Promise Test

Psychological Corporation
Testing Time: 90 minutes
Grades: 6–9

This test provides a broad and differential description of a student's abilities. The areas this test measures are: *Abstract Reasoning, Numerical, Verbal,* and *Language Usage.* The total score represents the academic promise of the student.

Differential Aptitude Tests

Psychological Corporation
Testing Time: 181 minutes
Grades: 8–12

These tests were developed to provide an integrated, scientific, and well-standardized procedure for measuring the abilities of students, both male and female, for the purpose of educational and vocational guidance. This battery consists of 8 tests designed to measure 8 different abilities, which are: *Verbal Reasoning, Numerical Ability, Abstract Reasoning, Space Relations, Mechanical Reasoning, Clerical Speed and Accuracy,* and *Language Usage,* which includes *spelling* and *sentences.* Each test is an independent test with its own administration and norms. This allows any or all of the tests to be administered to a student.

General Aptitude Test Battery

United States Employment Service
Testing Time: 135–180 minutes
Grades: 11–12

The objectives of this series of tests are to measure those factors that have been found to underlie job success and to develop occupational norms and validity data for those factors. In this way, it is possible to test all significant aptitudes in one testing session and to interpret a person's score in terms of a wide range of occupations. This battery now includes 12 tests which measure 9 aptitudes. The 9 aptitude scores obtained are: *Intelligence, Verbal Aptitude, Numerical Aptitude, Spatial Aptitude, Form Perception, Clerical Perception, Motor Coordination, Finger Dexterity,* and *Manual Dexterity.*

GROUP ACHIEVEMENT BATTERIES

California Achievement Tests

California Test Bureau
Testing Time: 2 hours and 58 minutes
Grades: 7–9; 9–14

This test is designed to measure the basic skills and learning functions at each grade level. There are three subtest areas, each divided into two parts: *reading* includes reading vocabulary and reading comprehension; *arithmetic* (junior high) or *mathematics* (high school) includes arithmetic reasoning and fundamentals; and *language* covers both mechanics of English and spelling.

Iowa Test of Educational Development

Science Research Associates
Testing Time: 7 hours and 39 minutes
5 hours and 39 minutes
Grades: 9–12

This is an achievement test consisting of a battery of nine objective tests designed to provide a comprehensive and dependable description of the general educational development of the high school student. The subtests included in this battery are: *Understanding of Basic Social Concepts, Background in the Nat-*

ural Sciences, Correctness and Appropriateness of Expression, Ability to Do Quantitative Thinking, Ability to Interpret Reading Materials in the Social Sciences, Ability to Interpret Reading Materials in the Natural Sciences, Ability to Interpret Literary Materials, General Vocabulary, and *Uses of Sources of Information.*

Metropolitan Achievement Test, Advanced Battery

Harcourt, Brace & World, Inc.
Testing Time: 4 hours and 35 minutes
Grades: 7–9

This battery measures student achievement in the important skill and content areas common to the junior high school curriculum. The author's intent was to develop tests that would contribute most effectively to teacher understanding and analysis of pupil achievement. The battery is divided into 10 subtests, as follows: *Word Knowledge, Reading, Spelling, Language, Language Study Skills, Arithmetic Computation, Arithmetic Problem Solving and Concepts, Social Studies Information, Social Studies Study Skills,* and *Science.*

Metropolitan Achievement Tests: High School Battery

Harcourt, Brace & World, Inc.
Testing Time: 5 hours and 15 minutes
Grades: 9–13

A series of measures of achievement in language arts, social studies, mathematics, and science. Eleven subtests yield the student's achievement in: *Reading, Spelling, Language Arts, Language Study Skills, Social Studies Skills, Social Studies Vocabulary, Social Studies Information, Mathematical Computation, Mathematical Analysis and Problem Solving, Scientific Concepts and Understanding,* and *Science Information.*

Sequential Test of Educational Progress

Educational Testing Service
Testing Time: approximately 8 hours
Grades: 7–9; 10–12

The purpose of this achievement battery is to measure education in terms of the student's ability to apply his school learned skills in the following seven areas: *Reading, Writing, Listening,*

Essay, Social Studies, Mathematics, and *Science.* These subtests are designed to measure general outcomes of education rather than specific course content.

Stanford Achievement Test, Advanced Battery

Harcourt, Brace & World, Inc.
Testing Time: 3 hours and 45 minutes
Grades: 7–9

This battery includes eight tests in a single 32 page booklet. The tests are *paragraph meaning, spelling, language, arithmetic computation, arithmetic concepts, arithmetic applications, social studies,* and *science.* The cover on the test booklet has space for all pertinent data about the student as well as his grade score, percentile rank, and stanine for all eight subtests. A Partial Battery of this test is also available (all of the above tests with the exception of the science and social studies tests). Some of the tests are also available as separate booklets.

Stanford Achievement Test: Advanced Modern Concepts in Mathematics Test

Harcourt, Brace & World, Inc.
Testing Time: 50 minutes
Grades: 7–9

This test is designed to provide a measure of the current objectives of a modern mathematics program. The test contains 64 items measuring student knowledge or skills in number skills and numerations, geometry and measurement, operations and number properties, mathematical sentences, factors and primes, sets, logic, symbols and definitions, graphs, tables, probability, and statistics. It is suggested that the use of local norms be considered in interpreting scores from this test because of the unstable nature of the modern math curriculum, diversity of method, and the practice of introducing the program at different levels of the curriculum.

Stanford Achievement Test—High School Battery

Harcourt, Brace & World, Inc.
Testing Time: 5 hours and 20 minutes
Grades: 9–12

This battery contains parallel titles to the Stanford Achievement Test, Advanced Battery. These are: *Reading, Spelling, English, Numerical Competence, Mathematics, Social Studies, Science,* and three additional tests in *Arts and Humanities, Business and Economics,* and *Technical Comprehension.* These tests are designed to cover the areas of education needed for productive development of all students. (See Chapter 10 for examples of test questions.)

Stanford Diagnostic Reading Test

Harcourt, Brace & World, Inc.
Testing Time: approximately 2 hours
Grades: 4–8

This is a diagnostic test used to expedite identification of student weaknesses and strengths in basic reading skills. This test measures six skill areas, which are: *Reading Comprehension, Vocabulary, Syllabication, Sound Discrimination, Blending,* and *Rate of Reading.*

Test of Academic Progress

Houghton Mifflin Company
Testing Time: 5 hours and 30 minutes
Grades: 9–12

This test is a multilevel test battery which includes six subtests for each of grades 9–12. The subtests are: *Social Studies, Composition, Science, Reading, Mathematics,* and *Literature.* These tests were designed to provide an efficient and comprehensive appraisal of student progress toward the most commonly accepted goals of secondary school education.

GROUP INTEREST INVENTORIES

The Gordon Occupational Check List

Harcourt, Brace & World, Inc.
Testing Time: 20–25 minutes
Grades: 11 and 12

The content of this check list is specifically relevant for the young man or woman who will leave high school to enter the world of work and who will need guidance in identifying from among the large number of existing occupations those which may be appropriate to his or her interest and ability. It is self-administering, with no stated time limit. The student puts his responses on the six page folder. The check list attempts to measure interest in five major occupational areas: *Business, Outdoors, Arts, Technology,* and *Service.*

Holland Vocational Preference Inventory

Educational Research Associates
Testing Time: 30 minutes
Grades: 9–12

This is a brief inventory about a student's feelings and attitudes toward various kinds of work. The results are computed on the basis of 11 scales: *Realistic, Intellectual, Social, Conventional, Enterprising, Artistic, Self-control, Masculinity, Status, Infrequency,* and *Acquiescence.* The raw scores of the student can be computed and transferred onto a profile chart. High peaks represent a student's favorite methods or desirable roles and situations, and low points represent the opposite.

Kuder E General Interest Survey

Science Research Associates
Testing Time: 45–60 minutes
Grades: 7–12

This is an interest survey primarily for the purpose of vocational counseling. The survey booklet has 168 questions. Each question states three different real-life activities. The student taking the inventory indicates which of the three activities he likes most and which he likes least. The following interest areas are measured by this scale: *Outdoor, Mechanical, Computational, Scientific, Persuasive, Artistic, Literary, Musical, Social Service,* and *Clerical.* The student's scores in each of these interest areas are placed on a profile sheet for interpretation.

Kuder Occupational Interest Survey, Form DD

Science Research Associates
Testing Time: approximately 30 minutes
Grades: 9–12

The Occupational Interest Survey consists of 100 triad statements. The student marks a most preferred and a least preferred activity for each triad. The person taking this inventory is expected to answer all 100 triads and to answer them as though he can do all the things listed. The items are not designed to have any obvious occupational relevance, but they do appear to differentiate among many occupational groups. Seventy-nine occupational scores and 20 college-major scores are reported for men; 56 occupational scores and 25 college-major scores are reported for women. The women's score also includes 32 scales developed on male subjects.

Minnesota Vocational Interest Inventory

The Psychological Corporation
Testing Time: 45 minutes
Grades: 9–12

This inventory provides information on the interest patterns of men in nonprofessional occupations. It is designed to help counselors who are working with students who are thinking about going into occupations at the semiskilled and skilled levels. For each student who takes this inventory, scores are derived to give an index of similarity between his interests and the interests of men in many of the nonprofessional occupations. The items are drawn mainly from Navy manuals and civilian trade descriptions.

Strong Vocational Interest Blank (Revised)

Consulting Psychologist Press, Inc.
Testing Time: 45–60 minutes
Grades: 12

The Strong Vocational Interest Blank is used to identify the distinction among various occupations sought by college students. This is accomplished by establishing a similarity between a person's interest and those of successful men (or women) in each occupational area measured. The purpose of this inventory is to help guide students into these various occupational areas. There are 54 occupational choices for men and 32 occupational choices for women.

Index